A PHOTOGRAPHIC GUIDE TO DOGS WITH JOBS

WORKING DOGS AROUND THE WORLD

MAS · YANKA & KING · STAR · A J & RACHEL · PETRO · SNOOPER · BRUNO · SWEEP · BUSTER · WOLF · HAPPY RALPH · MEL · KAVIK · ELMER · ENDAL · CAYENNE · WILLIE · HONEY HURRICANE · FLINTIS · CRICKET · TAMMY

MAS (Newfoundland) ▪ Brivio, Italy PAGE 3
Italy's premier water rescue dog

YANKA AND KING (German shepherds) ▪ Bosnka Kruppa Bosnia PAGE 15

Bosnian land mine—sniffing team

STAR (black Labrador) ▪ West Midlands, England PAGE 25
England's first arson-detection dog

A J (bloodhound) AND RACHEL (weimaraner) ▪ California, U.S.A. PAGE 37
Pet detective team locates missing animals

PETRO (German shepherd) ▪ Florida, U.S.A. PAGE 47
Disaster search-and-rescue dog

SNOOPER (beagle) • Florida, U.S.A. PAGE 57
Professional termite-locator

BRUNO (German shepherd) ▪ Connecticut, U.S.A. PAGE 67
K-9 police dog

SWEEP (Border collie) ▪ Gloucestershire, England PAGE 81
National Sheepherding Champion

BUSTER (Australian cattle dog) ▪ Kingaroy, Australia PAGE 93
Life-saving cattle herder

WOLF (borzoi) ▪ Edmonton, Canada PAGE 107
Superdogs performance jumper

HAPPY RALPH (greyhound) • Quebec, Canada PAGE 117
Star racetrack athlete rescued from certain death

MEL (poodle) ▪ Ontario, Canada PAGE 127
Muscular, manicured, and Best in Show

KAVIK (malamute–timber wolf) ▪ British Columbia, Canada PAGE 139
Wolf dog actor hits the big screen

ELMER (Alaskan husky) ▪ Anchorage, Alaska PAGE 153
Iditarod sled-dog champion (on right)

ENDAL (yellow Labrador) · Hampshire, England PAGE 167
Highly trained graduate of Canine Partners for Independence

CAYENNE (Labernese) • Quebec, Canada PAGE 181
Seeing-eye dog and companion

WILLIE (golden retriever) ▪ Michigan, U.S.A. PAGE 193
Predicts epileptic seizures

HONEY HURRICANE (cocker spaniel–retriever) ▪ Nova Scotia, Canada PAGE 203

Brings warmth and companionship to nursing home residents

FLINTIS (Anatolian shepherd) ▪ Namibia, Africa PAGE 217
Protects both his flock and its predator, the endangered cheetah

CRICKET (Jack Russel terrier) ▪ Andersen Air Force Base, Guam PAGE 227
Protects the environment against marauding brown tree snakes

TAMMY (Border collie) • Cape Town, South Africa PAGE 237
World's first marine protection dog, Eco-Agent A1142

DOGS

WITH

JOBS

DOGS
WITH
JOBS

WORKING DOGS
AROUND THE WORLD

Merrily Weisbord *and* Kim Kachanoff, D.V.M.

POCKET BOOKS
New York   London   Toronto   Sydney   Singapore

Photo credits appear on page 248.

 POCKET BOOKS, a division of Simon & Schuster Inc.
1230 Avenue of the Americas, New York, NY 10020

ISBN: 0-671-04735-3

First Pocket Books hardcover printing April 2000

10 9 8 7 6 5 4 3 2 1

POCKET and colophon are registered trademarks of
Simon & Schuster Inc.

Book design by Lindgren/Fuller Design

Printed in the U. S. A.

For our family and all mothers and daughters
who touch each other's hearts and funnybones
with their minds.

Contents

Preface: Nellie and Kim / xi

Introduction: A Celebration of Senses and Instincts / xiii

CONTENTS

PART FIVE: SERVICE DOGS

PART SIX: ECO DOGS

Preface

Nellie and Kim

At first we couldn't see her. She was in a wooden cage, and when she jumped up against the side, one of the planks fell away. We found her cowering. She was motionless, scared, tail between her legs, looking up at me with her beautiful amber eyes. What struck me first was her vulnerability, but shining out through the fear were her bright eyes, radiating intelligence.

I was six and I wanted her.

She was my dog. My first dog.

Around us in the dirty, crowded kennel, her unhappy companions barked wildly. The man said this small dog, furry from a winter outside in the cold, was half Saint Bernard and was going to be huge.

We bundled her into the car, me holding her tight, and got her home. As soon as the door opened, she escaped, tearing down the road. I called and called, thinking she had run away. She came back, right to me, and never left again.

She knew she'd been adopted.

Apart from my grandpa, Nellie was the deepest bond I'd ever known. From my sixth birthday to when I was eighteen, Nellie was my best friend. I was a solitary country kid, but I never felt alone because Nellie was always with me. Together we explored woods, caves, and streams, and I didn't worry about getting lost: Nellie was nearby; she would protect me. When I brought home my first boyfriend, she wouldn't let him hug or kiss me—she was watching over me.

I decided to become a veterinarian because of Nellie. I wanted to make sure she was well and I wanted to be able to heal any illness she might have.

Nellie's one bad habit was chasing cars, and I couldn't break her of it. Years later, after she lost her winter fur and hadn't grown any bigger, I realized Nellie was a collie cross. By chasing cars she was following her herding instinct.

Nellie died in my arms when she was thirteen. Her legacy was to imprint on me the profound, enriching meaning of the human–animal bond. Nellie blessed me with her instinct and intelligence. Had she fully realized her herding potential, she would have protected and cared for entire flocks, as one of human beings' exceptional allies, the working dog. Instead Nellie chose to love and protect me as her full-time job, and the abiding memory of her devotion inspired this book.

Dr. Kim Kachanoff

Introduction

A Celebration
of Senses and Instincts

Since the days of the first shepherds tending their flocks, dogs have worked as accomplished herders, guards, and hunters. Today, dog jobs are far more plentiful, fascinating, and diverse. Our modern dogs rescue, entertain, sniff out land mines, protect wildlife, and nourish humans, body and soul.

Dogs and people develop the strongest rapport when collaborating closely or working hard together. Over time, good handlers learn to appreciate and respect their dogs' profound abilities. Connected intuitively, a dog-and-handler team develops a special trust that is key to releasing each dog's astounding potential. Very often, these highly trained animals outperform both humans and machines, making them the perfect choice for their chosen jobs. In the case of arson, Labrador retrievers surpass modern detection equipment; beagles routinely beat out high-tech mechanical machines to discover termite nests; German shepherds clear life-threatening land mines faster and more safely than any human; and no person can match a Border collie's ability to herd sheep.

It's wonderful how perfectly suited dogs are to being "man's best friend." And the key to their helpful, companionable nature lies largely in the senses and instincts they inherited from their ancestor and prototype, the wolf. So genetically similar are these two canines that the American Society of Mammalogists classifies the domestic dog, *canis familiaris,* as a subspecies of the wolf, *canis lupus*. Dogs and wolves can even mate and produce fertile off-spring—and no DNA test can tell them apart.

The divergence between dogs and wolves began about 135,000 years ago. As wild wolves started venturing near human camps for food scraps, our ancestors developed an appreciation of wolves' social organization, hunting skills, and protective nature. They noticed that some cubs were naturally friendly, and others were wild and unapproachable. The more domestic, trainable cubs were allowed to thrive and the others were driven away or killed. This marked the beginning of basic breeding.

Through continued contact with wolves over the centuries, humans recognized the wide range of wolves' abilities. They saw that some wolves were superior trackers, hunters, runners, or swimmers; some possessed keen hearing and would warn of approaching enemies; and others were naturally protective of children. Humans bred these "helpful" wolves with other wolves of similar talents, reinforcing their valuable traits in successive generations. This was the beginning of primitive breeds.

As humans traveled the world, they continued breeding the best with the best and arranging canine trades with other clans. Over time, this breeding technique—pooling specific genes for specific characteristics—had its desired effect. Tamer wolves and their packs became less like their original wild ancestors and increasingly bonded and useful to human beings. Today, there are more than two hundred officially registered dog breeds worldwide and close to another two hundred non-registered breeds. Big, small, furry, sleek, Saint Bernard or Chihuahua, they all trace their ancestry back to the wolf.

Today, dogs are an integral part of our society—humanity's first, most durable, and most delightful achievement in domestication.

SENSES

Smell

A dog's perception of the world is a unique marvel, shaped in large part by highly developed senses inherited from its wolf ancestors. With two hundred million nasal olfactory receptors, a dog's sense of smell is one thousand to ten thousand times more effective than a human being's. Smell is the dog's most acute sense, the primary tool used to search for food or share information.

Dogs innocently sniffing each other's behinds, or urinating on a fire hydrant, are actually communicating through odors. They inhale minute chemical molecules that dissolve in their nasal mucosa, bind to protein receptors, and produce a signal that begins a remarkable journey along the olfactory nerve to the brain. From a single drop of urine, the sniffing dog learns the marking animal's sex, diet, health, emotional state, and even whether it's dominant or submissive, friend or foe.

Since odor molecules fly off objects all the time, dogs can be trained to find almost anything, even people. Humans shed thousands of skin cells every minute, and when these cells and other body secretions are broken down by bacteria, the resulting gases give each of us a unique scent. Tracking dogs follow a biochemical trail of dead skin cells, sweat, odor molecules, and gases, a sort of invisible bread-crumb trail that only they can see. For them, a scent article is like a three-dimensional "odor image," much more detailed than a photograph is for a person. Dogs can track a scent through snow, air, mud, water, and even ash. Canines truly see the world through their noses.

Hearing

Wolves depend on their sense of hearing for communication and hunting. Their universe revolves around the pack, but wolves must search for food over vast distances and are often separated from each other. Keen hearing and far-reaching howls are the links that bind the pack together. Even from very far away, the wolf can distinguish every nuance of another wolf's distinct howl, relaying danger warnings, reunion calls, and hunt details— the long-distance communication that ensures the survival of the pack.

Dogs inherited their ancestors' acute hearing, their most developed sense after smell, again, far superior to its counterpart in humans. Not only can dogs hear faint sounds over great distances, they can also pick up high-frequency sounds inaudible to humans. A hertz is a unit of measurement applied to sound frequency: One hertz equals one cycle per second, and humans are limited to hearing sounds in the 20–20,000-hertz range. Frequencies greater than 20,000 hertz, called ultrasound, exceed the human hearing limit, yet dogs can hear frequencies up to 67,000 hertz. Dogs hear the high-frequency "silent" dog whistle loudly, while humans can only perceive a faint hiss. They also easily pick up the ultrasonic sound waves emitted by flying insects, crickets, and voluble rodents.

Working dogs rely on their exceptional hearing to do their jobs: Herding dogs react instantly to subtle, distant changes in voice pitch, commands, and whistles; guard dogs stay tuned for any threatening rustle or creak; and service dogs respond to their master's softest whisper.

Sight

A dog's vision is a fascinating amalgam of enhanced and restricted abilities. For example, dogs can see in much dimmer light than humans, an ability also possessed by their nocturnal ancestors. While both dog and human retinas contain the same two types of photoreceptors, a canine's is composed primarily of rod photoreceptors and a human's is made up mainly of cone photoreceptors. Rods are better for dim light, while cones enhance detail and color vision.

Dogs also have a tapetum lucidum, a highly reflective layer of cells located behind the retina, which adds to their superior low-light vision. By reflecting light back through the retina, the tapetum lucidum doubles the photoreceptor's opportunity to react to each quantum of light. It also makes a dog's eyes, when illuminated at night, appear to glow.

Due to their wide-set eyes, dogs' total field of vision exceeds that of humans—250 degrees, compared to 180 degrees in humans. With this enhanced peripheral vision, dogs are always aware of everything going on around them. They are also far better at detecting motion than humans. Alertness to movement is especially evolved in various sight hounds, who can distinguish moving objects from more than half a mile away.

Yet surprisingly, dogs are less visually acute than humans, meaning that they are less able to discern fine details. Most dog owners discover that their

dogs can't recognize them at a distance until they identify their gait, hear their voice, smell them, or get close. Their dogs see someone moving but can't distinguish facial features. Dogs' visual acuity is only 20/75, which means that a dog needs to be within twenty feet of an object to see it clearly, whereas a person can see it sharply at seventy-five feet. Dogs also have difficulty focusing on objects closer than one foot from their eyes, while children see fine detail at three inches. For objects that are very near, dogs rely on their sense of smell or taste for proper identification.

Dogs do possess color vision, but not to the same extent as humans. Cone photoreceptors, responsible for color vision, make up nearly 100 percent of the center of a human retina, but less than 10 percent of a dog's. Dogs are likely to see color primarily in shades of blue and yellow, much as color-blind people do. However, dogs are better than people in differentiating among subtle shades of gray, which further enhances their low-light vision.

Like humans, some dogs see better than others. Some are nearsighted, some are farsighted. These traits can be inherited and it is possible to breed dogs for improved eyesight. Sight hounds, such as greyhounds, whippets, and borzois, have been bred for centuries to chase swift game by sight. Retrievers, like the Labrador and Golden breeds, watch their masters' hand signals and visually track falling birds. Herders, like the Border collie and Australian cattle dog, respond to their stock's, or handler's, most subtle movements. Actor dogs heed the crook of their handlers' fingers or the lift of an eyebrow. Guide dogs use their sight to become the "eyes" of their visually impaired owners.

INSTINCTS

The ways in which dogs use their remarkable senses can be attributed to their instincts. Dogs are born with strong behavior drives inherited from their wolf ancestors. Some dogs have strong instincts to follow scent, some are natural guard dogs with strong protective instincts, and retriever-type dogs instinctively pick up objects in their mouths. Formal training then reinforces these instincts, producing dogs supremely well suited for their specialized work.

The Pack Drive

Dogs' pack instinct comes from wolves, who live together in small groups of extended family members. The pack shares cub-raising, and the older wolves teach the young to hunt and behave. Individual wolves vary in the strength of their instinct to dominate or submit, establishing a clear social hierarchy within the group. The "alpha" male is the pack leader.

Communication is vital to pack harmony, and wolves use a wide variety of sounds and other sensory signals to understand one another. They bark, howl, growl, yip, whine, lick, smell, and are finely attuned to body language—

the movement of ears and lips, posture, the angle of the tail, warning gestures, and courting gestures.

Sensitive dog lovers also watch their dogs' body language and know that their dogs are constantly reading humans' often unintentional signals. Wolves' survival depends on divining the pack leader's guidance. With dogs, humans have become the "pack." A well-socialized dog accepts its owner as the leader, or alpha wolf: Its strongest desire is to please, obey, and be with its master.

Dogs with a high pack drive, such as service dogs and search and rescue dogs, solicit petting and play, enjoy grooming, like to touch, and would scale mountains to fulfill their leader's wishes. Their sensitivity to body language tells them when someone is suffering or hurt, and they instinctively come in close to comfort and protect.

The Prey Drive

Wolves must hunt, chase, and forage for food, but the domestic dog no longer needs these prey-drive behaviors. This instinct still surfaces in dogs that stalk pet cats, herd bicycles, and hunt, pounce on, and kill their toys.

A strong prey instinct is essential for detection dogs, police dogs, hunting dogs, and herders.

The Defense Drive

The defense drive derives from the wolf's territorial imperative to guard its den area from predators. Dogs with a strong defense drive are self-confident, hold their tails aloft, stand their ground, and guard their territory, family, and sometimes even their toys and food. They tolerate petting and grooming but don't really enjoy it. A healthy defense drive is desirable and most prevalent in guard dogs.

The Flight Drive

The flight drive is also a defensive drive, strongest in dogs that lack self-confidence. A dog with a high flight drive is unsure in new situations, holds his tail low and between his legs, may hide behind his owner, is stressed when he is separated from his owner, crawls on his belly or urinates when repri-manded, and may bite from fear when cornered. Dogs with high flight drives generally do not make ideal working dogs in any field.

Particular breeds of dogs show tendencies toward certain drives, but, as with all living beings, there are many individual exceptions. In general, Anatolian shepherds, Karelian beardogs, rottweilers, Doberman pinschers, and German shepherds are guard breeds, expected to be high in both prey and defense drives, moderate in pack drive, and low in flight drive.

Golden retrievers, Labrador retrievers, standard poodles, and other companion breeds are expected to be high in pack drive and moderate in prey and defense drives. They make excellent guide and rescue dogs.

Border collies and Australian cattle dogs usually have high prey and pack drives, moderate defense drive, and a low flight drive. They are ideal herders.

Millions of pet owners bask daily in the comfort, pleasure, and joy dogs bring them as companions and friends. But few know the potential of their canine companions' senses and instincts, and the strength of their dogs' desire to please. The following real-life dog stories from around the world celebrate the amazing gifts of dogs with jobs. Here you'll find dogs who warn people of oncoming seizures and save them from certain death by detecting land mines; dogs who guard flocks from hungry predators and protect the ecosystem from smugglers and snakes; dogs who specialize in the detection of arson evidence and termite infestation; and dogs who give sight to the blind and strength to those in need. These dogs mean something extra special to their partners—and to all who cross the threshold into their remarkable worlds.

PART ONE

SEARCH AND RESCUE
&
DETECTION DOGS

MAS

It's warm and clear on the shores of the Ligurian Riviera and Mas, a big black Newfoundland, takes a break from her patrol to sneak a sniff at the fishermen's morning catch. Further out on the ocean, fierce winds from the Gulf of Tigullio have begun to lift and swirl the surface of the sea, but the beach remains calm.

Mas and her inseparable companion, Ferruccio, scan the horizon and observe a fleet of multicolored sailboats heading toward port. Instinctively, both focus on one fifteen-foot boat desperately struggling to maneuver upwind. Turbulence and rough waters thwart the inexperienced sailor's attempts to dock, forcing the boat toward the sharp rocks on the wrong side of the breakwater. The crew scrambles to set the sail, but Ferruccio can see they are not going to make it. He quickly clambers along the slippery rocks to the end of the jetty, Mas close on his heels, barking excitedly. The pair work their way to the farthest, safest launch point, and leap into the angry waves.

Momentarily disoriented in the pounding surf, Ferruccio reaches out for Mas. At the feel of her master's hand, the enormous black dog sets out swimming strongly, clearing a path through the waves to the floundering craft.

Newfoundlands are dogs of the sea, equally at home on land or in water. In the Canadian coastal province from which they take their name, they were the constant companions of fishermen who wouldn't leave port without them. The dogs pulled heavy fishing nets out to sea, hauled carts filled with the day's catch, and rescued drowning seamen. In heavy seas, they proved invaluable for carrying the mooring lines to land and pulling heaving boats to safety.

Descended from the Tibetan mastiff, the Newfoundland crossed the Bering Strait during the late Ice Age with North America's original settlers. Archaeological remains show that the Newfoundland's forebears worked as sled and water dogs alongside Native Americans many centuries before John Cabot's exploration introduced European dogs into their gene pool.

The European continent "discovered" Newfoundlands in the nineteenth century. In an inscription on his dog's monument, Lord Byron immortalized his Newfoundland, Boatswain, "who possessed beauty without vanity, strength without insolence, courage without ferocity, and all the virtues of man without his vices." In France, the breed was used to patrol the river Seine in Paris.

Most Newfoundlands' coats are a deep, rich black. Other color combinations—Irish setter brown, charcoal gray, and the black-and-white combination known as the Landseer, named for the painting of a Newfoundland by the English Romantic artist Sir Edwin Landseer—are the result of crossbreeding with European dogs brought by the first colonists.

Newfoundlands are large and powerful enough to pull a man or boat to safety. Females stand twenty-five inches at the shoulder and weigh 115 pounds. The male stands around twenty-eight inches at the shoulder and weighs 150 pounds. In addition to their great strength, size, and endurance, Newfoundlands possess additional physical attributes that make them excellent water dogs: webbed paws, with a highly developed membrane between the toes to give their powerful swimming stroke an extra boost; a muscled tail, to provide a strong rudder; and a water-resistant double coat, fine underneath and shaggy and oily on top, to keep them warm and dry. So endowed, the Newfoundland can survive icy water rescues that might prove fatal to other breeds.

A Day at the Beach

Eleven-year-old Mas pokes her broad, good-natured face out from under the large kitchen table that barely conceals her massive bulk. Gently but persistently, she nudges Ferruccio for a share of his brioche. After a decade in the family, Mas, the matriarch, has a privileged position. Ferruccio chuckles softly. Dakota, the junior at seven years old, waits politely for her share of the sweet breakfast roll. The two highly trained water rescue Newfoundlands have settled comfortably into family life with Ferruccio, his wife, Elsa, and their daughter, Valentina. "When we go somewhere, they come with us," says Ferruccio. "When we go to the cinema, they come along. We would like to visit England and Scotland, but until they lift the quarantine, we won't go, because we won't leave Mas and Dakota behind."

Ferruccio bought Mas from a breeder in Bergamo when she was just a two-month-old ball of black fluff. In his work as a volunteer firefighter, he had met rescue dogs and was impressed by the legends of the Newfoundland's exploits, and by their gentleness, courage, and enormous strength. Even as a

puppy, Mas showed the great rescue instinct and enormous desire to work inherent in her breed.

"Come on, Mas, let's get in the car, we're going to the lake," Ferruccio calls. At the sound of these magic words, Mas knows it's a work day. She rushes to the door, almost taking the table with her.

The family squeezes into their Opel station wagon stuffed with rescue gear, harnesses, wet suits, fins, life jackets, and backpacks. In 1989, Ferruccio Pilenga inaugurated the first Italian school for canine lifeguards, Scola Cani Salvataggio. He and his canine inspiration, Mas, teach and train dogs and handlers for nautical rescue. In addition to the standard rescues, they have perfected a unique canine helicopter rescue technique for inaccessible, heavy seas. Every weekend, under the expert guidance of Mas and Ferruccio, eager disciples hone their dogs' lifesaving skills and instincts. Today's drive to Brivio, on the river Adda, will take an hour, just enough time to rehearse the training schedule and make the final cell phone arrangements for boat and helicopter transport.

Fifty dog and handler teams are waiting to greet them at the river's edge, instructors dressed in red T-shirts and caps, pupils in blue. Mas's silhouette, the icon of the school, is emblazoned on all the gear.

Sixty yards offshore, a lone swimmer simulates distress and cries for help. Caught in the violent current of the Alpine river, his head bobs up and down as he fights for air.

The thrashing swimmer kick-starts Mas's rescue instinct, beginning today's training exercises. The charge of adrenaline washes away her advanced years. No longer is Mas Ferruccio's favorite "old lady." She barks energetically and strains toward the river.

On the embankment, a training group of seven massive Newfoundlands whimpers and squirms in puzzlement, looking at their handlers and each other, uncertain what is expected of them. Mas surges toward them, dragging her teammate, Ferruccio, behind. She assumes her place of command at the water's edge and, barking wildly, rears up on her hind legs and pulls toward the swiftly moving waters.

Mas's infectious enthusiasm inspires the other dogs and, one by one, the confused pupils begin to bark. Loud yips and yelps soon reverberate along the riverbank as the novices take their cue from the old veteran and focus on the struggling swimmer.

With a great leap, Mas hurls herself into the fast-flowing water, Ferruccio close behind. The weight of her body pulls her under but she quickly resurfaces, nose first. Head held high, she checks for her partner, then powers through the waves to the drowning man. Avoiding direct contact, she slowly circles the exhausted victim, a technique she and Ferruccio developed. "It has," Ferruccio explains, "a calming and tranquilizing effect."

Gratefully, the swimmer grabs on to Mas's red-and-yellow harness. Ferruccio quickly joins them, rolls the weakened victim onto his back, and hooks his arm over the man's gasping chest and under his armpit in a secure lifesaving hold. If the victim had been unconscious, Mas would have taken his hand or wrist gently in her mouth and begun towing. Now Ferruccio supports the man's head above water, taking over his grasp on Mas's harness. Buoyed by the towline, Ferruccio can reassure the victim or immediately start artificial respiration if needed. Without the help of a dog, precious lifesaving moments are lost and a drowning swimmer can lapse into a coma in the water before onshore resuscitation is initiated. "We're a team," thinks Ferruccio, feeling the power of Mas's strokes, "and when it comes to water rescue, two is better than one. Having a friend to count on is very important."

Confidently and powerfully, Mas tows her two charges to shore.

Ferruccio pulls the swimmer out of the river, the "victim" dons his school sweatshirt, and Ferruccio pats and cuddles his favorite bundle of wet fur. The assembled students clap in appreciation. Yapping short sharp barks of pleasure, Mas romps and rolls on the embankment like a puppy, basking in the purest, most perfect reward she knows—praise and affection from her owner. Ferruccio's wet suit is put to the test as she returns his affection with slobbery Newfie kisses of undying love.

Now it's Elsa's turn to slip into the water upstream. She swims forty yards out and begins struggling and crying for help. As a further test of their rescue instincts, the future lifeguards are lined up on shore—this time without Mas's motivating presence. As they watch Elsa flailing, initial consternation and puzzlement gradually give way to one isolated bark, then another. Sheer pandemonium soon breaks loose as the assembled Newfoundlands strain and pull, yelping and barking, all rescue instincts on full alert. Their handlers jump into the water and, inspired by regal Mas's example, the younger dogs enthusiastically follow suit. "Mas has a lot of energy, which she transmits to the other dogs," Ferruccio says. "They see her leaping without fear, and even dogs that hesitate will dive from the pier." Ferruccio calls this "imitative learning" and it is an integral part of his school's innovative methodology.

. . .

The history of Italian water rescue is the history of Mas and Ferruccio, and the core of their school is the bond and trust between them. "We base everything on the teamwork between the dog and its master," Ferruccio emphasizes. "We teach teams various intervention techniques, how to swim together in perfect harmony, and how to help each other in turn." His water rescue school is the only one in the world to pair dogs routinely with their handlers in the water. The French and Swiss schools use a different method, sending their dogs into water rescues alone. These schools first teach the dogs to retrieve objects in the water, then to retrieve people. "But in our school," Ferruccio says with a laugh, "we throw the dog's owner into the water first. Our dogs don't do anything their owners don't do first and so trust is built."

Mas achieved the highest French, Swiss, and Italian water rescue certifications by performing progressively difficult aquatic feats: diving off high piers; rescuing a drowning person in breakers on a rocky shore; swimming a mile to a drowning victim and towing him to safety; towing master and victim aboard a boat to shore; and riding a floating object to perform a rescue independently. Mas's ultimate trial was in Venice, in 1989. The skeptical Italian coast guard agreed to test the young Newfoundland's lifesaving abilities. Unlike France and Switzerland, Italy had never used dogs as part of its water rescue program. As a coast guard volunteer simulated drowning, Mas courageously leapt from a rocking motorboat straight into water rescue history. This daring feat earned her an official water rescue accreditation from both the coast guard and the harbormaster. Mas became the first dog ever to achieve this honor in all of Italy. "But it was the inaugural helicopter rescue Mas performed for our school's highest certification that heralded a different type of work," says Ferruccio.

. . .

Teachers and pupils watch the sky above the Adda as a helicopter swings low over the swiftly moving mountain river. Mas barks expectantly from the bank. The next training stage is the hardest, but it is also her favorite.

A "victim" enters the strong current and swims out into the river.

The roar of the helicopter is enough to terrify most dogs, but, from the beginning, Mas reveled in this experimental form of water rescue.

"We followed orders from the police pilot," Ferruccio remembers. "Mas climbed in and out of the helicopter with the motor off a few times. Then we stayed aboard and they started the engine. She quickly got used to the din, and the noise of the running motor became part of the game for her." In many situations, boats cannot quickly reach the scene of water emergencies, and helicopters offer the speediest solution. "The first time, the dogs just fly in the helicopter. They don't jump, only their masters do, so we don't traumatize them with the helicopter," Ferruccio explains. "We must teach them step by step. If the dog is fine flying, the following time they can dive."

Before Mas and Ferruccio came along, canine helicopter water rescues had never been attempted.

Now the whirring blades add to Mas's excitement. Waiting on shore, she barks wildly at the sight of the swimmer struggling in the river and at the sound of the landing helicopter, two compelling calls to action. Keyed up, but with the utmost control, she boards. The helicopter is small and any undisciplined movements could put them all in jeopardy. With her long black coat brushed by the wind and her muzzle lifted to the sky, Mas fully enjoys the exhilarating ride.

The helicopter banks sharply, positions itself, and hovers six feet above the swimmer below.

Mas readies herself in the jump position on the special anti-slip carpet. Her muscled hindquarters bunch for maximum momentum. Undeterred by the spray, wind, and choppy waters, she launches herself out of the hovering helicopter and into the churning river below. Her heavy body and head submerge completely. Then she pops up, her first thought for Ferruccio, who has jumped in, straight-legged, behind her. Other dogs jump in after their handlers but, as always, Mas leads the way. As soon as she locates her master, she swims to his side. Together, they stroke toward the thrashing victim.

When Mas and Ferruccio first started experimenting with helicopter water rescue, Ferruccio used a cable winch to lower them together into the water, judging it the safest technique. Then one day they were assigned to a helicopter without a cable. Ferruccio's commander friend suggested that the pair dive directly from the helicopter. That first free fall was Ferruccio's most moving moment with Mas.

"We were alone and there wasn't anyone to help us. The dive was from a high altitude, nine to twelve feet. Mas was fantastic. She jumped out before I did without hesitating her first time. She demonstrated that it was possible to do it."

Back on shore, a new crop of dogs learns to approach the deafening helicopter. Ferruccio observes them closely, knowing there is a secret about Mas that none of the others knows. Her old body is now arthritic. The fearless dog that helped him appreciate the incredible potential of rescue dogs can now barely walk up steps. Yet, in the water, she is rejuvenated. "When it comes to training and it's time to work, Mas has amazing energy, even if she has passed her ten-year mark," Ferruccio says. She no longer works as a lifeguard, patrolling the beaches and shores of Italy. Mas is a teacher now. But Ferruccio will never forget her days on active duty and the lives she saved, especially that day in the stormy surf off the Ligurian coast.

Mas was already waiting for him in the water when Ferruccio surfaced. The waves were high and he was glad to have her by his side as they swam

together toward the wind-tossed sailboat. He knew Mas could handle the surf, but the young sailors could not. They were scared and panicky, futilely attempting to set the sails and start their outboard motor. On one side, the sailors saw the looming, jagged rocks; on the other, a man in a red wet suit with an enormous black dog leading him through the waves.

Mas swam toward them with strong, efficient strokes.

Ferruccio remembers shouting, "Throw the line to the dog," using all his might to yell above the swell.

Frustratingly, the young men hesitated, terrified to throw away their lifeline to a dog.

"Trust her, trust her," he screamed, pointing to Mas circling in the rough breaking waves.

Finally, with no choice but the sharp limestone or the dog, the frightened sailors tossed the rope in Mas's direction. The bowline arced high, landing close to the big Newfoundland. Fighting the lashing breakers, Mas pounced and clamped the line securely in her strong jaws. Relieved, Ferruccio signaled her to swim out to the open sea. Reaching deep with her large paws, Mas pulled powerfully away from the rocks. Slowly, the boat spun about and, to the amazement of the frightened sailors, buffeting winds filled the sails. The mast creaked and the sailboat shot off toward safe, open water.

Ferruccio is still thinking of Mas's past glory as the helicopter blades whir and young four-legged trainees happily throw themselves into the green waters of the river Adda. Now Mas's strong desire to save lives blossoms in new generations of Newfoundlands groomed for water rescue. Ferruccio smiles to himself to see her very important role continue. In the years to come, Mas's students will grow more numerous, an extended pack of aquatic rescuers ready to assure the safety of all the major ports and beaches of Italy. They will carry on her pioneering spirit, soaring above the waters—courageous Newfoundlands, dogs of the sea and of the air.

BOSNKA KRUPPA, BOSNIA

YANKA AND KING

Strong, lithe Yanka sniffs the grass on the mist-shrouded hillside beside the school. Despite the morning chill, her handler, Chris, sweats under his thick protective visor, on full alert. Lines of wooden stakes strung with white ribbons demarcate the landscape as far as the eye can see. Taller posts hold up red-and-white signs. Blazoned on each are a skull and crossbones.

A cock crows a wake-up call somewhere in the village, but Yanka and Chris have already been on the job for an hour. King, the bushy-coated third member of the team, patiently waits his turn in the back of a nearby transport truck.

Chris wears a bright blue Kevlar vest and matching visored helmet designed to protect his head and vital organs in case of an explosion. The week before, on a nearby minefield, a metal detector caught a trip wire and detonated a land mine, killing a deminer. The dogs wear no protection at all.

An ambulance with paramedics waits on standby.

Suddenly, Yanka begins to sniff and snort loudly. She comes to an abrupt halt, motionless in the innocent-looking field, eyes glued to the ground. Chris's body tenses. He moves slowly along the safe corridor toward his dog and inches forward for a closer look.

Yanka and King are two highly trained explosive-detection German shepherds. Together with their handler, the young South African deminer Chris Boshoff, they form an expert land mine detection trio. Now on contract to the non-governmental Bosnian agency Akcija Protiv Mina (APM), the team has been based in the war-ravaged village of Bosnka Kruppa for the past six months.

German shepherds' courageous temperament, impressive strength, and large size, as well as their adaptability to different climates, make them ideal for military and police operations. They have also proven particularly well-suited to the rigors of land-mine sniffing. During World War II, the Korean War, and the Vietnam War, land-mine sniffer dogs were deployed on a limited basis. But in the 1989 Russian evacuation from Afghanistan, land-mine detection dogs began to play an important role in reclaiming potentially deadly, unusable land.

With the proliferation of land mines came the need to establish safety standards and controls for mine detection dogs. All detection dogs working in Bosnia must achieve one hundred percent accuracy in compulsory land-mine detection tests or undergo further training.

Demining is big business—it's estimated to cost five dollars to put a land mine in the ground and one thousand dollars to remove it—and demining dogs are an increasingly hot item. In accuracy trials conducted by the U.S. Department of Defense, land-mine sniffer dogs, used in conjunction with traditional methods, proved the most successful way to unearth hidden mines. For every land mine found with a metal detector, there have been one hundred to two hundred false positives. But detection dogs are much more accurate. Their highly developed olfactory abilities allow them to scent the TNT

enclosed in traditional metal land mines, and even to sniff through the plastic casings of newer mines, which often foil modern mechanical detection devices.

Chris is "hard" on his dogs, exercising them at midday and pushing them to their limits. Every afternoon, they practice searching for deactivated mines, honing their skills and receiving praise and rewards when they make a find. To keep his two dogs concentrated and dedicated, he uses only one at a time, alternating them every half hour. Chris feels the weight of the responsibility he and his dogs bear for the lives of the villagers and his deminer friends. "I don't want any of them to step on a mine behind my dogs."

A Clear Playing Field

Standing stock-still in the minefield, Yanka stares intently at the ground in front of her. Then, with a quick shake, she forges ahead, tail waving, nose to the ground. Nothing there. The relief in Chris's posture is almost tangible. The agile two-and-a-half-year-old German shepherd continues her search with puppy-like enthusiasm. She moves up and down the taped-off square on the hillside, employing a zigzag search pattern to ensure thorough coverage.

Before Chris and his dogs begin to search a "box," demining personnel must painstakingly establish a safety zone around it from which Chris works. The deminer, or sapper, moves around the perimeter of the square delicately flicking a handheld wire rod across four inches of ground at a time, feeling for hidden trip wires. Trip wires are attached to mines such as the Yugoslavian-manufactured PROM, designed to explode and spray six hundred shards of shrapnel at the velocity of speeding bullets. The deminer then cuts the vegetation and scans the perimeter with a metal detector. If there is a hint of a positive response, he inserts a long probe into the soil at a precise thirty-degree angle every inch—the width of the smallest type of land mine standing on its side. Bosnia is particularly challenging and dangerous to demine, due to the constant shifting of front lines that occurred during the three-year war. By war's end, neither Serbs, Croats, nor Bosnians were able to provide definitive mapping of the minefields.

Standing in the safe corridor on the outer edge of the box, Chris feeds Yanka lengths of leash to accommodate her movements in the uncleared box.

This is Yanka's first assignment and she is protected by a new clearance method being tested in Bosnia. Since it's not proven that dogs can detect trip wires, the boxes she searches are never larger than the expected trip wire's length. The trip wire of the live PMR-2 Alpha land mine found earlier in this field was 20.4 yards. The area Yanka is working is only twelve yards square, so Chris is assured that the sappers would have picked up any longer PMR-2 trip wires before Yanka went in. Chris is careful to avoid allowing the leash to touch any part of the ground—it takes only eighteen ounces per square inch to detonate a mine.

"*Soek!* Search!" he says, directing her in Afrikaans. She obeys, thoroughly investigating every blade of grass, every tuft of dirt.

"Don't look there!" She speeds up and dispenses only a passing sniff at the ground underfoot.

On the mortar-damaged roof of a farmer's home, a visored sentry in a blue vest stands watch. He holds a walkie-talkie, ready to call in a mine removal crew if there's a find.

On the plateau below Chris and his dogs, the large white school building stands silent and empty. Soon, for the first time since the war ended five years ago, it will ring with the voices of hundreds of young Bosnian children. The structure has been declared mine-free. But Yanka, King, and Chris are working on the hill beside it, which was a strategic Serbian artillery position during the war and is still an active minefield. There are a million hidden land mines in fields like these scattered throughout the twenty thousand square miles of Bosnia.

Yanka and King, along with other land-mine detection dogs, have cleared tens of thousands of square yards of land. So far, in Bosnia, there is only one incident in which a dog detonated a mine—a far better safety record than that achieved by humans.

The sentry's radio crackles to life, cutting the silence and concentration. Yanka has been working for twenty minutes and has once again widened the area of habitable land. It's time for a break.

"*Kom hier!*" Chris calls. "Come here!"

Tail still wagging, Yanka follows Chris's directions to the safe zone.

"Heel," he commands as soon as she reaches his side.

"Sit. Stay," he orders, his tone urgent, acutely aware that any spontaneous movement could threaten their lives. Only when Yanka's leash is securely attached to a stake does he relax and remove his stifling visored helmet.

"You beauty!" he tells her, ruffling her fur affectionately.

At the transport truck, Yanka hops obediently into her familiar crate. She is greeted by an anxious whine from the adjoining cage—dark, thick-coated King, eager for his turn in the field. Unlike Yanka, the nine-year-old, gray-muzzled veteran was not initially trained by Chris. King had already uncovered hundreds of land mines in Zimbabwe before they met.

But King's past served to create a special bond between him and Chris. Back in South Africa, Chris heard that King was about to be put down due to a mysterious pain that occurred when he was sniffing for land mines. Taking the initiative to have King properly X-rayed, Chris discovered that a bone splinter originating from the German shepherd's nose had lodged itself in his jaw. After surgery, King was as good as new and happily back on the job at Chris's side.

King strains at the leash, trying to pull Chris toward the uncleared boxes. "He's got a very sharp nose. He knows what it's all about. Sometimes, if you don't stay ahead of King, King will go ahead of you. He's definitely his own man." With his robust build and long-haired coat, there's something almost bear-like about King.

Chris ties King's lead to the side of the truck and kneels beside him, hugging and caressing.

"Good boy," he murmurs.

Having a second dog for "quality assurance" lets Chris sleep well at night. "In some circumstances, Yanka is actually better than King, and vice versa. King prefers working in bushy areas, whereas flat open areas are Yanka's specialty." So far, the two have not had a difference of opinion when it comes to their final verdict on a cleared area.

King's body wags and undulates with frantic enthusiasm. He can't quite reach the rubber Kong toy on a string that Chris is swinging in front of his face. Again and again, Chris ricochets the Kong, a durable rubber toy used as a reward or incentive for working dogs. He tantalizes King, bringing out his prey drive, "to get him focused on the Kong and then on the explosives."

When King's prey drive has reached its peak, Chris walks abruptly to the taped-off search area and pretends to toss the Kong into it.

"We make as if we've thrown the Kong into the square, so he'll go into the square thinking he's going to get his Kong but instead he finds the scent of the explosive. He knows he'll get the Kong as a reward soon after."

Returning to King, Chris displays his empty hands.

"*Waars hy nou?*" he asks. "Where's it gone?"

Quickly attaching the furry shepherd to a second, longer leash, Chris leads him to the square, where the Kong has "disappeared," and aims a kick at the perimeter. "To get King interested in the minefield and searching, I had to make it fun for him, so I would cover his eyes and then kick the Kong into the search area. Then I took the Kong away and just kicked at the grass. He seems to like it and gets really worked up when I do it." Playtime is important for strengthening the trainer-dog bond, and also gives Chris important information on how to read his dogs. "It's the small things he does that actually give me an indication of whether he's found the mine or not."

The rising sun has burned off most of the early morning mist as King sets to work. Today, he's beginning a new square in the field near the school, and tomorrow Yanka will provide her expert second opinion. The day, which promised to be cool, rapidly heats up, a hazard to King's powers of concentration and endurance, given his hirsute bulk.

Sabahudin Hodzic, twenty-six years old, balances on his artificial leg, watching from safe ground as King works. In October of 1994, while walking on a footpath near his home, he was knocked over by a blast. "A couple of seconds later, I felt and saw that I had lost my leg." Sabahudin knows firsthand how potentially hazardous King's work is and is grateful for the service he provides.

King lumbers up and down the square, tail flopping easily from side to side as Chris observes from the safety zone, a required thirty feet away. Chris's visor begins to fog up with the humidity and the heat. His eyes follow King working the box. He watches his dog's sniffing intensify and his movements concentrate in one small grassy area where the smell is strongest.

Then, like a heartache, he sees it happen.

King sits down on his tail, looks over at Chris, and yawns. This laid-back alert is his lifesaving signal. Unlike other detection dogs, who alert by pawing and scratching, King stays quiet to avoid detonating the live mine. He's made a find!

King stays still, panting softly. He looks at Chris, then looks down at the ground in front of him. This is the crucial moment when one false move by King, one happy bounce or impromptu ear scratch, could kill or severely maim them both.

Chris signals the rooftop sentry, who relays the alert through his walkie-talkie. Then he maps out the exact location and he and King walk back carefully to the deminer and show him where the alert took place. The demining crew moves in and carefully deactivates the live PMR-2 before removing it to a safe area for detonation.

By 11:00 A.M., it's quitting time, too hot for the dogs to work. Chris finds a tennis ball for a game of fetch. He throws it far into the river, and King swims out to retrieve the prize. Chris immerses himself in the cool, welcoming water and calls his dogs to join him. He's proud of them. It would have taken twenty deminers all day to clear the five squares—seven hundred and twenty

yards—that Yanka and King have reclaimed today. And King's find has once again proved the value of all well-trained, certified land-mine detection dogs. Chris floats on his back, relaxing, as the dogs frolic leisurely in midstream.

Back in the quiet suburb, an admirer drops by to visit the German shepherds. Chris lets Yanka and King out of their roomy enclosure in the backyard to say hello to Sabahudin. The visitor explains that he has come to pay tribute to the dogs who risk their lives for him and his fellow villagers. He pats them affectionately and coos to them in the universal language of endearment.

A horse and buggy pass by on the road below, signaling a return to normal life. The sound of hammering resonates from the village rising from the ashes. Chris is pleased to note that "whenever the dogs finish, people go back to their homes, plant vegetables, put up roofs, and start rebuilding their lives. You can see they actually trust us, and that's pretty gratifying." He looks fondly at his two admirable dogs, knowing that soon, because of them, children will once again laugh and play safely in the reclaimed field beside the school.

· · · · · · ·

WEST MIDLANDS, ENGLAND

STAR

Four soft paws fitted with leather Paw Boots pick their way carefully through a scarred burn site. A pair of black rubber boots follows behind, sloshing through the sodden debris. A wall cracks, a broken beam hangs by a nail, the ceiling creaks. Fire Inspector Clive Gregory and his dog, Star, are the only living beings in the burned-out house.

Nose to the ground, Star sniffs, Clive's beam lighting the way. He pads past charred couches and clothes, around gaping floorboards. Fast and agile, he searches purposefully, sniffing every nook and cranny of the chaotic debris.

Minutes into his search, Star's body tenses. Ears forward, tail waving, every cell in his muscular body strains to locate the elusive scent only he can detect.

Star, a four-year-old male black Labrador retriever, is Europe's first fire investigation dog, "a pioneer," says his master, Fire Inspector Clive Gregory. Working together since 1996 in the West Midlands Fire Service, Star and Clive form an inseparable team. "The bond between us is unique," says Clive, a specialist fire investigator for the past seven of his twenty-six years in the fire service. "We have trained, worked, and lived together since he was a puppy and he really does think of me as his dad."

With the incidence of arson in the United Kingdom doubling in the past decade, totaling forty percent of all fires, Star's addition to the fire investigation unit has proven invaluable in solving arson crimes. In half the fires he has investigated, Star has detected arson. All his finds have been later confirmed by gas chromatography techniques at the forensic laboratory.

There are now more than two hundred canine accelerant detection teams operating in North America and six in the U.K., thanks to Star's success. As Clive says, "Star shows just how useful a dog can be to man, what an absolute asset. A working dog does the job that he is trained for far better than a person could do it. Star can find substances that humans and electronic equipment fail to detect. There are numerous occasions when I use him, thinking it's a hopeless case, and—bingo—he comes up with a find that I didn't think was there."

Hot Evidence

Star's day starts at dawn. Clive is awake, stirring somewhere inside the house. His wife, Marjorie, and their two pet dogs are still asleep. Star sits patiently outside the patio doors. He's been there the past two hours, waiting so that, on yet another day, he can lean in close against his sandy-haired, good-looking, forty-eight-year-old master, the source and focus of all love and affection, the one who reassures him and gives direction to his life.

Hearing car keys, the rustle of a coat, and the sound of Clive putting on his boots, Star quivers with excitement. When Clive opens the door, Star is on him like a ton of bricks. Paws on Clive's shoulders, he licks the familiar mustached face, nuzzling him with his cold, long snout.

Clive has had Star since he was a five-month-old pup. He has seen him grow from an awkward, gangly adolescent to a sleek, muscular, finely tuned professional search dog, the best Britain has ever produced. Clive trusts Star's instincts, depends on him, and appreciates him for his keen, enthusiastic nature. He reaches out to calm Star, "fussing" his dog just the way he likes. He strokes his broad head firmly, pats and scratches his ears, and speaks softly with the slow, gentle voice Star loves, feeling how loyal and totally bonded Star is to him. It is a trust he could never betray.

"Let's go," he says as they approach the Land Rover, vigorously thumping Star's flanks to key him up for work. Seemingly on springs, Star leaps high off

the ground, bounding, and jumping. Clive knows his dog wants to please, to do his job. All Star's training involved positive feedback, using a reward system based on praise and play. One of the reasons Clive loves working with Star is because he's such a happy dog, always keen to work. For Star, play is work and work is play. It's all a game.

Clive opens the door to the back of the modified Land Rover and Star leaps eagerly into his metal transporter, leather booties and red tracking harness hanging from a hook. The Land Rover pulls out, its license plate, appropriately, K9.

The K-9 arson unit drives through Birmingham, past council housing, to a smoldering block of masonry flats. Outside, suited firemen roll up their hoses, tenants huddle desolately on the periphery, and a lone reporter waits to see if the blaze was caused by arson. The fire chief briefs Clive. The firemen have found rolled carpets laid against the doors of the burned flats, and a terrified man found hanging out the window, screaming to be rescued, has been taken into custody. The fire chief asks Clive if the canine team can investigate.

First Clive goes in alone. Using a high-beam flashlight, Clive carefully inspects the site for loose floorboards, open shafts, glass shards. He also checks for burning, or hot, embers, making sure, as always, that nothing could hurt or injure his dog. Star's safety is paramount to Clive, and although he knows Star is crucial to the investigation, he would never expose him to danger.

Reassured, Clive goes to fetch Star. He advises the fire crews to hang back because Star hates noise. Panting with anticipation, Star watches him approach. Clive unlocks the transporter and unhooks Star's harness and paw boots. Star doesn't like the boots, but tolerates them when necessary. He lies on his side, gazing trustingly up at Clive as he fastens the four Velcro ties. With his red search harness in place, Star leads Clive into the main landing of the doused building, past collapsed beams, directly to a pile of rolled-up carpets against the door of the first flat. Clive watches Star's nose and body

language, waiting for him to come across an incriminating substance floating in a vapor cloud or a scent blowing downwind. He watches him search until, sniffing the carpets furiously, tail wagging at high speed, Star zeroes in on a folded center section of carpet. Moving quickly into the sit position, tail wagging in glee, he looks up at Clive with a wonderful alert look on his face as if to say, "I found it, boss, I found it."

"You're such a clever boy, a good lad," Clive enthuses.

He pulls out Star's toy rubber ring and all play breaks loose—tug and pull, toss and catch. Star wriggles happily, mouth open in a doggie grin, replete with praise, play, and affection from Clive.

A crime officer bags the find to bring to the laboratory. As Star and Clive exit past the suspect in police custody, Star shows an avid interest in the man's left shoe. He sniffs intently, then sits in the "alert" position, surprising even Clive with his unexpected find.

In the station, at the request of the police, Clive has Star perform a line search including some of the suspect's clothing. He identifies the same shoe for the second time and, once the items are rearranged, locates the shoe again. The laboratory confirms the presence of gasoline both on the carpet and on the shoe, and eventually the suspect is convicted. This arson case is closed.

Star's amazing ability as an arson dog stems from a combination of his natural canine olfactory prowess, superior genetics, intensive training, and responsive nature. Molecules of odor fly off objects all the time and, like other dogs, Star's sense of smell is thousands of times more sensitive than humans'. Even minute particles of odor molecules are captured and amplified in his nasal mucus, membranes sending signals to his brain. Star's training has encoded a "vocabulary" of ten different hydrocarbons into his memory bank: gasoline, paraffin, acetone, diesel, turpentine, cellulose, lighter fluid, white spirits, mentholated spirits, and barbecue fuel. Substances produced naturally during a fire are not part of his vocabulary. Unlike Star, mechanical devices can't distinguish between naturally produced fire substances and arson accelerants, and so they often produce false positives. Since these natural substances are not part of Star's vocabulary, the only alerts he gives are for true arson accelerants.

"Star is more efficient than the latest high-tech equipment," Clive has discovered. "He can find substances that machinery can't and is much faster and more mobile than any machine. Sometimes a fire is so intense the substance is burned away and machines are unlikely to register it, but Star can pick up the scent."

A fire burns cozily in the canine team's office in the West Midlands fire station. A sign on the door reads FIRE RESEARCH AND INVESTIGATION. Four cluttered desks, labeled file folders, greeting cards pinned to the wall, charts, one blackboard listing fire fatalities, and another listing suspected arson incidents investigated by Star surround Clive, who is busily writing his morning report. Star is resting near the door. Seeing Clive occupied, Star creeps along the floor toward him. "Stay," Clive commands, deepening his tone. Star hesitates briefly and creeps forward again, testing the boundaries. Clive looks down at his report, at his partner, Star, and groans in resignation. Recognizing an opening, Star bounds forward, rear end wiggling happily, and flops onto his back, four paws in the air, for a blissful chest and tummy rub.

The phone rings. The fire chief from Stourbridge, in the West Midlands back country, has a problem: Three days ago, a building was set on fire deliberately, an investigation was held, a man is in custody, but all the debris has been cleared from the building without finding any sign of accelerant. The man later confessed to starting the fire with gasoline. The problem is, with no evidence to corroborate the crime, the man can withdraw his confession at any time.

"Could you and Star come have a look?"

"It's a hopeless case," Clive warns. "But we'll give it a try."

At the fire scene, Clive finds the house totally gutted. Furnishings trashed, staircase demolished, floorboards carboned over, black and deeply charred.

Clive doubts there is anything left to find. He looks down at Star, whose expressive eyes are asking for a chance to do his job. Clive knows Star's search dog pedigree is impeccable. Star's sire is an explosives search dog on active service in the Middle East, as are all his uncles. His dam was an explosives search dog and her sisters work in narcotics detection. Clive remembers training with five-month-old Star at Karenswood (International) Ltd Kennels, Worcestershire, where Star was born and raised with his dam, now retired. In the 1960s, kennel owner Alan Sims created a training system for hydrocarbon search dogs that attracted little interest in the U.K. and was reluctantly exported to the United States. The first U.S. arson dog was trained in 1986. Ten years later, Clive and Star brought the system home.

Labradors make good search dogs because they are well accepted by people and they have a gentle nature, but Sims and Clive could see Star had something more. Clive remembers choosing him over his brother because of his "biddable" nature, "not just obedient, but it matters to him, and he takes notice of everything I require him to do." Unlike a dominant dog, who would be more likely to challenge authority, Star wanted nothing more than to please Clive. Following the principle of "one handler and one dog," they began training intensely together for three months. Gradually, Star learned to identify and differentiate between the different hydrocarbons—under rocks, diluted, buried in earth, and hidden in progressively difficult situations. He also learned to "relate" or "signal" his find by sitting down beside the found substance. Clive constantly reinforced young Star, encouraging, praising, rewarding, and creating their unbreakable bond.

· · ·

Now, in the dark, gutted house, Clive looks down at Star. He knows Star will do anything in his power to please him, even what seems impossible.

Putting his trust in his dog, Clive sends Star in.

In front of the fire crew, the police, the crime investigator, and a dog handler—in-training, Star begins his search around the perimeter, nose to the ground, tail at half-mast. Almost immediately, he zeroes in on a smell, his body language suggesting he is looking for something specific. Tail higher, waving, body more focused, he moves into the center of the room and stops. Tail wagging like a metronome, he looks up at Clive and deliberately makes two diagonal scratches, with his right and left paws, forming a cross with his claw marks. Then he sits at attention and puts his nose down at the center of the cross. "Good boy," Clive thinks, but, unconvinced, rewards him cautiously. He calls Star away and asks a fireman with a crowbar to crack the floorboarding. Under the floorboards, to the amazement of all the assembled witnesses, including Clive, they find gasoline. It had soaked into the floorboards, which had then charred over. The char formed a natural filter, destroying all the surface accelerant. Minute traces were retained in the surviving floorboarding, masked by the char, and Star had found the evidence.

"Such a clever lad," Clive exults, pulling Star to him, patting and hugging his dog with pride. "You found it and we couldn't."

Star grins with joy. He's so happy his whole body wags along with his tail.

At home, Clive gives Star a thorough wash, lathering, and scrubbing, while Star repeatedly attempts to return the favor by licking Clive's face. Black Labradors are the breed of choice for arson detection because their short coat is durable, easy to groom, and offers good protection in grimy, wet, and often harsh working conditions. Dirt dissolves. Star shakes. Droplets fly off him like pearls, drenching a laughing Clive.

Clive cleans up inside while Star, outside, watches him through the picture window. Clive tends to his two pet dogs, a Samoyed and a bearded collie, feeding them dog food mixed with leftovers. The dogs eat and wander off to lie down in the living room. Clive brings Star dog food, without leftovers, to prevent him from being distracted by human food smells at burn sites. Star eats hungrily, and Clive smiles at the contrast between his pet dogs' independence and Star's reliance on him. Star is uninterested in playing with the other dogs, and despite Marjorie's fondness for him, he's very mischievous with her sometimes, ignoring her commands and taking liberties. Star is a one-man dog. Mealtime and sleep time are perhaps the only moments Clive's working-dog partner isn't in close physical contact with him, or watching his every movement.

Most days, Clive keeps Star in shape with varied, constantly stimulating daily training. He runs him through a regular obedience routine of sit, stay, call to a halt, catch the ball, and sit still when the ball is thrown away, then retrieve it on command. Often, Clive puts a selection of objects on the ground from which Star must identify the accelerant-scented item. He makes a game of it, sometimes combining these exercises with a search and find, constantly inventing new exercises, trying to "shake it up so as not to bore him." Star never really knows what they are going to do. Clive puts him in the sit position while he rummages around in the garage to find things to hide for him. "You can see the intensity; his ears are forward, he's watching, as if to say, 'What's he up to now?' I keep him guessing; that gets his mind thinking and makes it more enjoyable for him."

Today, after their hard day's work, training's on hold. It's time to relax and unwind.

Star sits beside Clive in the passenger seat of the Land Rover, going fishing. Clive plays Star's favorite audiotape, the soundtrack to "Dances with Wolves." Clive hums, Star howls along.

At water's edge, comfortably ensconced, Star watches Clive cast into the gentle running shallows of the river Tweed. Trees overhang the bank. The shore is quiet and devoid of people.

Under an umbrella in the rain, Clive, in full waterproof waders, casts futilely.

"Sure wish you were a trout detection dog," he teases Star.

Star rolls over trustingly, four feet in the air, tongue lolling to the side, and Clive scratches his belly affectionately, secure in the thought that he and Star will be together always. His agreement with the fire service is that when he retires, Star leaves with him. It is the right thing to do. Clive wouldn't want Star bounced from handler to handler like a piece of gear. Star will be Clive's permanent companion, and because of his dog's active mind and body and working-dog nature, Clive will always provide him with exercise and tasks. Clive believes Star is worthy of the best treatment there is, and he wants to give it to him. "He's mine for life," Clive vows.

· · · · · · · ·

CALIFORNIA, U.S.A.

AJ and RACHEL

AJ, a nine-year-old black-and-tan bloodhound, buries his face deep in the bucket, long ears safely outside, away from the food. He eats with the kind of bowl-'em-over concentration that is characteristic of bloodhounds on the trail, even though his owner and trainer, Kat Albrecht, is patting his flanks and tugging back the excess skin around his jowls. AJ doesn't look up; the only things visible are rolls of skin and those dog-food-free ears.

The phone rings and Kat answers How? When? Where? At her feet, her eight-year-old weimaraner, Rachel, raises her beautiful limpid brown eyes to gaze at her master. Kat gently caresses her soft, silky ears.

Then Kat is on her feet, collecting equipment, moving toward the door. "Come on, let's go," Kat calls.

The Pet Detective team is out the door.

· · ·

AJ and Rachel, retired from the police canine unit, and Kat, a thirty-seven-year-old ex–police officer, are the first official pet search and rescue team (PET-SAR) in the world. In the first months of their existence, they found more than two dozen lost pets and now they can't keep up with the demand from people whose pets are their main source of emotional sustenance. For these bereft individuals, the disappearance of a beloved pet is devastating, and their grief as all-encompassing as it would be for the loss of any loved one.

"Love is love," says Kat, "whether it's for a person, a cat, or an iguana, it is love. And when the source of what you love is missing, people want and deserve a professionally trained resource to come and help them."

In early 1997, Kat learned this lesson in spades. At the height of her police career as a bloodhound handler working with the SWAT team on criminal cases, specializing in search and rescue, her prize bloodhound, AJ, went missing. He had dug a hole under his kennel and disappeared, no doubt lured by a pungent trail. Suddenly, Kat was no longer a cool, controlled policewoman but a panicked pet owner. She had not only lost her pet, but her partner and friend, her baby. Frightened and desperate, she worried she would never see AJ again. She reacted quickly, calling a search and rescue colleague who was working with Thalie, a female golden retriever trained in scent discrimination. They gave the search dog AJ's bedding to smell and sent her out on AJ's trail. Within fifteen minutes, Thalie had tracked down AJ in the neighborhood around Kat's house, and Kat realized that dogs can not only understand the words "smell this pillowcase, find this person," they can also understand "smell this food dish, find this dog." Scent discrimination for finding people could also be applied to scent discrimination for finding pets.

After working together closely for years, depending on each other to do their police work well, little retraining was necessary for Kat and her dogs to transfer their search techniques from finding people to finding lost animals.

With time Kat had learned to trust her dogs' instincts and not mistakenly second-guess them, as she was prone to do at the beginning. Now she knows their signals intimately and heeds them. "My relationship with them is critical. They're my children, I can read them like a book."

And so AJ, Rachel, and Kat's PET-SAR team was born.

To the Rescue

AJ places his front paws on the back of the Jeep and Kat helps hoist the hind end of his hundred and thirty–pound body up into the cushioned transporter. Rachel, lighter and more agile, leaps up easily into the adjoining cage. Rachel nuzzles Kat with her velvety gray snout and AJ shows his affection with an accompanying wet slobber. The dogs watch Kat as she secures the door, eager and excited at the prospect of the day ahead.

The Jeep heads out, Rachel and AJ settled in the back. Kat's custom front plates promising:

MY SEARCH AND RESCUE DOG

CALIFORNIA

SURCH K9

NOSE IT ALL

Rachel was Kat's first search dog. Starting when Rachel was a puppy and continuing over the next three years, Kat trained Rachel in the new field of cadaver and body parts detection. Rachel worked for seven years before retiring from the police force. AJ, Kat's second dog, learned to trail missing people. He became a hero during his police career, finding a missing Alzheimer's patient, rescuing a lost hiker, leading police to burglary suspects, and earning the National Police Bloodhound Association Lifesaving Award for saving the

life of a suicidal man. After seven years' experience working with SAR dogs, Kat has complete faith in her canine partners.

If there's a missing pet to be found, this team will find it.

Kat drives quickly, remembering the panicked voice on the phone: "Bubba, my buddy, my baby, is missing. I need you to help me find my dog." She hears and understands, because it's happened to her. She wheels into a tree-lined residential street in Santa Cruz, hoping the scent is still strong after two days, knowing she's bringing aid.

Bubba's owner, Omar, a young, self-employed bachelor, paces impatiently as Kat dons a bright red vest announcing LOST PET RESCUE.

"He's a show-quality Jack Russell terrier, four and a half years old," says Omar, showing Kat a recent photo of an energetic little brown-and-white dog. "Wind blew open the side gate and he must have gotten out. Neighbors saw him go that way." Omar points east. "He's my life," Omar sighs, handing Kat his beloved dog's thick sheepskin blanket.

Rachel springs to life, fully alert when Kat pulls out her harness.

"Take scent," Kat commands, as both Rachel and AJ avidly sniff the scent the lost dog has left on the wool.

"Search," she says to Rachel, the dog chosen to first explore the terrain. Rachel is lithe, sleek, and luminescent gray, her loveliness evoking the Weimar folk legends of the "great gray hunting dog" and the "rare gray ghost." Her tail wiggles happily. She sniffs the air, "airscenting," searching for any olfactory trace of Bubba. She works in tandem with AJ, and her strength lies in determining the general area in which to concentrate the search. Later, if needed, AJ will be called in to narrow the field, following Bubba's unique scent along the ground, "trailing" his exact path.

Rachel bounds forward purposefully. She sniffs along the pavement, in the bushes, under balconies, at the sides of houses, moving at the steady, tireless weimaraner pace, covering one block, crossing the street, beginning another, searching thoroughly for any smell of Bubba. In nineteenth-century Germany, weimaraners were bred primarily to search for and retrieve birds and small game in the fields, forests, and in water. Rachel's bird-dog instinct is to freeze and point when she finds a live cat, unlike sight hounds, such as borzois or greyhounds, whose instinct is to chase down their prey. This instinct makes Rachel a natural pet rescuer, but training and intelligence are needed to overcome obstacles along the way.

Kat observes attentively as Rachel searches, waiting for a sign that she has picked up the trail. Omar, calling "Bubba, Bubba," follows closely on their heels. In the second block, on the corner of a groomed front lawn, Rachel's tail starts to wiggle frantically and her sniffing intensifies. Kat can see from her body language that Rachel is on a live Bubba scent.

Watching her happy, people-loving dog, Kat remembers the long years Rachel spent searching only for cadavers and body parts. Rachel loved her work, but Kat always knew she much preferred to "critter," the term used in search and rescue when a dog looks for rabbits, squirrels, birds, and other critters instead of people. Many times, when Kat was searching for a gun or a cadaver, Rachel would bunny hunt instead, and Kat would have to correct her. As a police dog, Rachel's inherited instinct to find game was a drawback. But for a Pet Detective, it was an asset.

Kat looks down at her fulfilled dog, reliving the pleasure of seeing Rachel blossom into a pet-searching dog. From the beginning of pet detective training, when she first gave Rachel the scent of a cat, "Rachel smelled it, smelled the fur, and looked up at me as if to say, 'You finally understand what I want to look for.' She absolutely loved it."

Rachel circles the yard repeatedly, on the scent but unable to take the trail any further.

Neighbors attracted by the brightly colored Pet Detective vests confirm that Bubba was seen in this yard the day before. Encouraged by the news, Omar calls louder and louder for his lost terrier.

Kat rubs Rachel's neck, Rachel looking up at her for the next command.

"Good girl," Kat croons, realizing this is as far as Rachel's airscenting abilities will take them.

It's time for reinforcements.

What's needed now is AJ's legendary bloodhound talent as an expert trailer.

AJ snuggles his head against Kat's waist as she pats his big head affection-ately, tugging on his long ears. "What a sweet, mellow, honest dog he is," she thinks. Soft-natured AJ bays and howls eagerly at the sight of his search har-ness. His back is level with her waist, so Kat barely bends to fasten the straps of her "little boy's" search harness.

"Get to work," she commands, and AJ, with the scent memory of Bubba clear as a photographic image in his brain, quickly picks up the trail leading out of the yard. Nose to the ground, excess skin folds almost covering his eyes, all AJ's sensory feedback is now funneled through his nostrils. He drags Kat along behind him, a one-track trailing machine, doggedly follow-ing Bubba's paw steps. As a bloodhound, AJ descends from the oldest scent hounds in the world. All scent hounds today are descendants of Saint Hubert bloodhounds, bred by French monks in the seventh century. Because of this finely tuned genetic selection, AJ and his breed have no equal in using olfactory capabilities for tracking or trailing. This, combined with Kat's intense search and rescue training—over the course of two years, four times a week—enables AJ to trail his quarry for miles, even if the trail is many days old. More amazing, and what distinguishes him and other bloodhounds from all other scent hounds, is AJ's enhanced ability to discriminate among odors. AJ can easily tell the difference between two people, or two dogs, or two cats, by encoding and remembering each indi-vidual scent.

AJ pulls Kat along, undistracted by children gawking, cars passing, Omar calling, or other dogs in his path. Kat recognizes his characteristic on-the-scent body language, "a camel walk, a certain waddle, a focused pace, head level with his body, never looking at me; I never see his eyes." She follows, proud of AJ's unshakable ability to concentrate on his work and pick up a lost trail. This is her reward for their years of training in

heat, cold, snow, at night, in helicopters, oceans, on mountains, in crowds, and in the traffic of busy parking lots.

Moving steadily in a loping walk, AJ covers one block, two, three, until he stops short, looks around, and looks at Kat, head turning right, then left, tongue lolling out of his mouth, a silly grin covering his face. "With that look on his face, I know he's lost the scent," thinks Kat. Then, shaking himself off as if to reset his smelling mechanism, AJ turns sharply and soon works his way back to the lost scent.

AJ's nose leads them from one yard to the next. Ignoring the jumble of odors all around him, he trails Bubba's distinct smell, unique as a fingerprint. His body tenses, his tail curls up. Soon, he accelerates, resolutely pulling Kat over lawns, flowerbeds, across streets, through picket fences, making a bee-line for a white suburban bungalow a few blocks away, until he arrives on the front step, stops still, and stares fixedly at the door. Kat understands AJ's signals and rings the bell.

A young woman in a jogging suit answers.

Omar, unable to contain himself, pushes past Kat and AJ, shouting, "Bubba, Bubba."

An ecstatic brown-and-white ball of fur launches itself through the open door of its temporary safe haven straight into Omar's arms. Wriggling in Omar's embrace, the little dog licks his owner's face over and over, tail beating, squirming in bliss. "Hi, my buddy, I missed you, I was so worried, I'm so happy you're back, my buddy, my friend," Omar cries with relief.

Standing quietly in the background, Kat rewards AJ with his favorite cheese treat. "Good boy," she says, the inflection in her voice changing, her pitch high and encouraging, rewarding AJ not by what she says but by how she says it. "You're my best little boy, aren't you?" she exclaims, scratching his ears and rubbing his chest. And AJ, the gentle giant, thumps his tail, snuggles into Kat, and drools appreciatively.

As working dogs, AJ and Rachel have already had two careers, serving as police dogs and most recently as pet detectives. Now it's time for the two old buddies to go home, slurp refreshing cool water, get hosed down, pass out, and dream doggie dreams under the shady fronds of a big palm tree.

As the rescue team heads home, Omar, reunited with his lost dog at last, reads the receding rear license plate on Kat's Jeep and chuckles with gratitude and relief.

GET LOST

SURCH K9

MAKE MY BLOODHOUND'S DAY

. . . .

FLORIDA, U.S.A.

PETRO

Creeping low, belly scraping the ground, Aly moves forward slowly. It's pitch black in the tunnel, but it's his nose that guides him, not his eyes. Ultra-sensitive nasal receptors follow a molecular trail of scent particles that waft in the air, like seeds from a dandelion. The smell grows stronger and Aly moves more quickly, ignoring the odors of rotting food and the stench of decaying corpses drifting up through the rubble. People cry, sirens wail, pigeons peck noisily at lifeless bodies. Aly blocks out the chaos. He has no time for distractions. The three-year-old dark German shepherd is on the job, in search mode, with a life on the line.

Crawling on her stomach in a hard hat, Caroline Hebard, founder of the U.S. Disaster Response Team, follows Aly closely, dog leading human on a mission of mercy. The night before, Miguel had pleaded with her, "Please come back to the factory with your dog before the bulldozers arrive." Nine days earlier, one of history's most powerful earthquakes had shattered the early morning rush of Mexico City, flattening buildings and killing thousands of people. Caroline and the American team of search and rescue volunteers had already checked this clothing factory, but Miguel was insistent. "Come soon, we hear voices from the building," he urged. Caroline reached down to pat Aly, who, she knew, was "feeling the stress of finding too many cadavers and not enough survivors." He looked back at her with his intelligent brown eyes as if to say, "Let's go, we're due."

A rat scurries near Aly's head and bizarre smashed forms loom in the darkness. Ten, twenty, thirty feet, and Aly stops at a rubbish pile. His excitement mounts as he begins to scratch and dig. He wheels around and his solid ninety-five-pound frame fills the beam of Caroline's flashlight. He charges playfully toward her, grabs the flashlight from her hand, and heads back out the tunnel. Caroline is left alone in the dark with no light, but she's smiling. Trained to self-reward after a find, Aly has dismissed himself to go and play. "He thinks the flashlight is a stick," she realizes. "He's got a live find."

Very soon after, two young women, barely clinging to life, are extracted from the rubble of the Mexican sweatshop exactly where Aly had alerted Caroline by grabbing her flashlight. The women say that after ten torturous days buried alive, it was hearing the dog's scratching that gave them the hope they needed to hang on just a little longer.

That day in Mexico, Aly followed a scent trail down thirty feet of a debris-strewn tunnel to earn the right to play with Caroline's flashlight. But the path that led to the Mexico City miracle is much longer and can be traced back, in part, to Aly's proud ancestry. Many dogs perform search and rescue (SAR) work, but none have been used as extensively, for everything from tracking to avalanche rescue, as German shepherds.

The first society to promote the breed was founded in 1889, and it remains the largest canine club in the world. The valor and versatility of German shepherds greatly impressed Allied soldiers in the First World War and, despite strict quarantines in the 1920s, large numbers were imported into Britain and the Commonwealth. Up until twenty-five years ago, the British referred to them as Alsatians or Alsatian wolf dogs to avoid anti-German sentiment.

Caroline Hebard travels to Germany to find her canine partners, believing that the breed can be found in its purest working form in its native land. Since the early 1970s, when she began her canine SAR work, the loyal, agile, and intelligent German shepherd has been her dog of choice. Aly's lifesaving Mexico City rescues took place in 1985. Today, sadly, Aly is gone, but his rescue instincts live on in Caroline's newest team member.

Now the torch has fallen to a brave young German shepherd—four-year-old Petro.

Nose for a Miracle

Petro wolfs down his bowl of kibble and oatmeal mixed with a sprinkling of canned dog food. He lies down, ever watchful, waiting to go back outside with his friend. He's already had his morning run-and-chase-squirrels play time with his mistress, who calls him "neat pooch" and knows that "enjoying play is important for a successful search and rescue dog."

Soon enough, Petro and Caroline are back in the fields behind her home looking for planted clues similar to those Petro would encounter when searching for someone injured or lost.

"Such!" Caroline says firmly, using the word for "search" that Petro learned in Germany. Bounding out where Caroline points, Petro crisscrosses back and forth across the field. Within minutes, he skids to a stop, barks, and lies down. Beside him is the wallet Caroline hid earlier. She scratches his neck and lets him have a quick tug on his Kong toy. Petro next finds a jacket, shirt,

and a set of keys, careful never to touch the evidence, leaving it intact for the investigators. After each find, he grabs the reward Kong furiously, showing his important "high prey-and-play instinct, excited about the prospect of playing with the Kong in almost a Pavlovian way. He thinks it's all a game."

Petro trots to his next "game," an obstacle course in Caroline's backyard set up to emulate a disaster site. He builds his confidence and agility as he burrows quickly through pipe tunnels, climbs up and over obstacles, and balances on beams that teeter like a seesaw. As he begins to cross a ladder joining two platforms, he hesitates. Caroline coaxes him, but Petro jumps off.

Without saying anything negative, Caroline simply commands him to sit and stay, and returns to the obstacle. Calmly she calls him back onto the ladder. Petro hops back onto the platform, then, gingerly, one careful foot in front of another, crosses to the other side.

"Yes," Caroline thinks, thumping his shoulder approvingly, "it's all about trust. He knows I will never send him into a place I wouldn't go."

Since Caroline first met Petro in Germany, when he was two years old, she has worked to strengthen the bond of trust that exists between them. She hid behind trees in Austrian forests with his rubber Kong and rode up ski hills in chairlifts with him at her side. Aly's first searches after his arrival in Florida were games of hide-and-seek with Caroline as the "victim," always carrying his favorite toy.

For Petro's last training exercise, in the woods, another SAR volunteer hides in the underbrush.

"Such and hilf," meaning "search and help," Caroline commands.

Nose low to the ground, the big shepherd follows the scent of hundreds of thousands of shedded human skin cells. The scent-detecting area of a German shepherd's nose is seventeen times larger than that of a human's, and Petro's especially long nose has earned him the nickname Moosehead. He follows the invisible gas trail formed by human skin cells, sweat, and other secretions as they are broken down by bacteria. He can smell this gas percolating through air, water, snow, mud, even porous concrete. But the large "docking area" for smells in Petro's nose is only part of his incredible sensing ability. The part of his brain reserved for interpreting the information relayed from his nose is also highly developed, and Petro's sense of smell is one thousand to ten thousand times better than a human's.

Caroline stands back and lets Petro do the work he does so well.

The "victim's" scent disperses downwind in a cone-shaped pattern, the smaller end centered around the person's body. As the distance from the source grows, the cone widens. When airscenting, it is Petro's job to locate the wide end of the cone and work back and forth until it narrows, leading him to the target.

Petro runs forward, stops, then heads back toward Caroline, searching for the strongest odor trail. He leaves the path, broad shoulders and powerful thorax pressing through the thick bush. In the woods, he runs almost a full circle. Suddenly, he hones in on a strong scent line and lets out a bark. Unlike Aly, who was trained to alert handlers by self-rewarding, Petro is trained to bark at a live find. Lying beside Petro, buried in leaves and brush, is the hidden "victim." Caroline pulls out the rubber Kong-on-a-cord and Petro tugs as though he's in seventh heaven.

After six months of intense daily training, Petro is "mission ready."

At 2:00 A.M. one day the following week, Caroline's beeper goes off. Petro's ears perk up in perfect isosceles triangles, "excited because he senses my adrenaline pumping." He registers Caroline's hushed tones as she receives a quick meteorology report from the coordinator of the Office of Emergency Management. An El Niño–energized jet stream has spawned deadly tornadoes and sent them skipping and crashing across four Florida counties, the deadliest outbreak in the state's history. The worst tornadoes, near Orlando, have already killed twenty-five people. Whole neighborhoods lie devastated in the wake of the two-hundred-mile-per-hour winds. Debris from trailer parks and other buildings is hampering rescue operations. Can Caroline come with her dog and help speed up the search?

Caroline remains calm but can't control the rush of energy coursing through her body. Sensing it, Petro begins to pace. He presses his nose against the house's sliding doors. When Caroline pulls out their emergency gear, Petro can barely contain himself. Now there are dozens of nose prints on the door. Caroline lets him out and in two huge bounds he's in the back of the Chevy Suburban, ready to work.

Caroline carefully packs water, food, flashlights, a tent. By 8:00 A.M., she and Petro are at the first site, a trailer park that once housed thirty homes.

Trailers lie on their sides, upended; water soaks strewn clothes and broken furniture; people mill about in confusion and distress.

As if he has been doing this for years, the novice Petro gets right to work. He weaves through the mayhem, sniffs over crumpled aluminum siding, and tunnels through collapsed trailers, his long hours of simulated disaster training actualized at last.

After a short search, Petro sounds a muted, cautious bark. Caroline recognizes her dog's "cadaver alert." She leads him away from rescuers and onlookers before rewarding him, knowing how delicate the situation is, wanting to reward her dog but painfully aware that "the people waiting to find out the fate of missing loved ones are about to have their worst fears confirmed."

For hours after this first find, Petro and Caroline search the damaged areas, making sure there are no more bodies or trapped victims. Quickly, Petro covers large areas that would take human searchers days to sift through. Efficiently, he "clears" the terrain so that worried relatives and friends can rest assured their loved ones are safe.

Rescue officials lead them to their last site of the day, the remains of a demolished hundred-unit condominium. Curious onlookers, concerned relatives, and rescuers look on as Petro trods carefully over the jumble of broken windows, walls, and furniture. Pieces of wreckage fly about in the strong wind. Caroline has trouble keeping up with her dog. She sees him stop, then disappear. When she catches up, he is in the wreckage of a child's bedroom, head under the bed, tail wagging.

This is not his standard "alert."

Caroline bends down to pull out Petro's find.

Two gerbils in a cage.

The crowd laughs and the tension breaks as the pets are reunited with a very worried little boy.

Caroline rewards Petro for the first real live find of his young search and rescue career. She scratches his ears, confident there will be many more to come.

Exhausted after a full day of searching and clearing, Petro and Caroline sleep soundly, camped in the Suburban. The next morning, at dawn, Petro investigates a wilderness area looking for a man missing since the storm hit. Onlookers protest, saying it is a waste of time to search so far from the man's house. But Caroline, heeding Petro's keen interest in the area, remembers an experience with Aly twenty years earlier on the Appalachian Trail. "Trust works both ways, and I've had some good teachers."

That brutally cold night, Aly taught her the importance of trust. Twelve children on a church-sponsored afternoon hike had disappeared on a section of the Appalachian Trail known as the Delaware Gap. When they hadn't returned by dark, the rangers called in Caroline and Aly. Aly quickly found the scent, then lost it briefly where the trail hit a road. The other searchers were convinced the children had turned right, or left, following the road. Surprisingly, Aly shot across the asphalt, straight into the woods. Caroline hurried after her dog, although everyone else was convinced he was on the wrong track. Thirty minutes later, Aly bounded back down the trail, a reward stick in his mouth, and led Caroline to twelve cold, wet, very relieved children.

Once again, in Orlando, searchers doubt her dog's abilities. But not for a split second does Caroline interfere, second-guess, or doubt Petro's growing concentration.

Minutes after disappearing into the brush downwind of a destroyed house, the big shepherd barks. Petro has found the man they're looking for, though, sadly, he is dead. It's a tragic discovery, but locating the dead bodies of their loved ones is crucially important to those still alive. Not until every-one has been accounted for can the living begin to deal with their grief and devastation. Petro's quick work allows the survivors to move on, literally and figuratively.

By evening, Petro and Caroline are on the road home. Caroline checks the rearview mirror and smiles affectionately at her dog resting in the back. Petro has done exactly what he was trained to do, located the bodies quickly, cleared the areas confidently, done his first job proud.

She pulls over a few miles down the road and sits on a rock while Petro stretches and unwinds. He comes up to her and lays his head on her lap, his intelligent brown eyes asking for approval.

"Finer hund," she whispers into his ear—*good dog.* She kisses him softly on his long snout, then looks down the highway to where clouds are breaking up for the first time in days. Shafts of moonlight leak down from the black sky. Caroline knows there will be other days when Petro will play just as important a role as today, but for higher stakes. Like the great Aly before him, Petro's work promises to save many lives, the miracle of canine search and rescue.

SNOOPER

Snooper stands up on the front passenger seat, the minivan door opens, and a blast of hot air hits her smack in the face.

"C'mon, girl, time to go to work," calls her partner encouragingly.

Snooper hops out into the ninety-degree Florida heat, trots across the lawn, and looks up fondly at her colleague, Kim Dunford. The Glens watch with worried expressions as the short-legged beagle and the businesslike twenty-seven-year-old woman approach jauntily across their lawn. At the door, Snooper raises her head to enjoy the full feel of Kim's scratching fingers. Dog and human eyes meet and Snooper sits calmly, waiting for her work to begin.

It's three P.M. and the working girls from Fahey Pest Control are right on time.

Seventeen years ago, the Wisconsin-born Glens cashed in their life savings and built their dream retirement home in the Grasslands residential development in Sarasota, Florida. Shortly afterward, uninvited guests invade the neighborhood . . . first the Wilsons down the block, followed by the Sterns next door. Soon, nearly everyone in their area was overrun by termites. But none of the Glens' three professional inspections had managed to locate any live insect invaders.

Now it's Snooper's turn to try.

The air-conditioning is shut off and the windows are closed to help Snooper's keen sense of smell detect trace odors of burrowing termites in the structure of the house. Kim runs her pointer along the baseboard.

"Find the Ts," Kim beckons.

Snooper pads alongside the wall, head low, moving her nose slowly from side to side.

Suddenly, the floppy-eared dog stops in her tracks. She pushes her nose into the floor and sniffs with a long snort. "She's in the zone," Kim thinks. "If anything's here she'll find it."

Snooper cocks her head and looks at Kim.

Search and rescue dogs, guide dogs, and police dogs may have more glamorous jobs than a termite-control beagle, but few have the dedication, focus, and upbeat attitude it takes to be a full-time nine-to-fiver. Similar small hounds were used for hunting in ancient Greece. But today's beagle is traced to the Norman Conquest of England, when the Talbot hound, a large tracking dog, was brought to Britain. This original foxhound was bred and selected to track, chase, and corner its quarry, alerting riders on horseback with its mournful bay.

Other Talbot hounds were selected and bred not to track, but for the convenience of their size. By the fifteenth century, texts refer to a small hunt-ing dog, never taller than fifteen inches high, bred to be carried in the pocket of a knight on a hunt. The name of these small hounds derived from the Celtic word *beag*, meaning small. Despite its diminutive size, the beagle quickly gained a reputation for its even, if stubborn, temperament and stamina.

For a while, in Victorian England, the ultimate in small hounds was a breed known as the pocket beagle, only ten inches in height. Queen Victoria and her consort, Prince Albert, owned a pack of these, which they carried to the country in a large picnic basket. By the 1880s, the trend in North America had shifted back to "larger" beagles. In 1888, the first National Beagle Club was established.

Sadly, the breed's clean, short coat, small size, and good nature have made beagles not only a favored pet but also the most popular breed of dog for medical research. Complete lineages of thousands of genetically pure beagles are bred solely for research purposes.

Today, beagles are popular hounds for unmounted hunters chasing small game, mainly rabbits. In many regions, beagle sales rise in direct relation to peaking hare populations. Throughout the centuries, perhaps because they are still bred for the hunt, beagles have maintained the strong work ethic that makes Snooper such a valuable employee.

Blue-Collar Beagle

Snooper sleeps soundly through Kim's beeping 5:45 A.M. alarm. When Kim opens Snooper's sleeper cage and pokes her face in, Snooper half opens her eyes, stretches out on her side, then goes limp again.

"C'mon, c'mon, girl," Kim urges. "Rise and shine."

Unmoving, Snooper listens to Kim's footsteps trudge up the stairs, down the stairs, and reenter the room.

"C'mon, sleepyhead. This weekend, we'll be on the boat!"

At the mention of the small cruiser with the bow where she loves to perch, ears flapping freely in the wind, Snooper finally rises and ambles out of the cage. As soon as Kim is out of sight, Snooper makes a beeline for the sun-filled guest room, flops onto the soft bed, and nods off again in seconds.

A wet tongue invades her dream world. She opens one eye to see Tina, Kim's other dog, a pet beagle, waiting eagerly. At Tina's friendly play-growl, Snooper finally gives in and gets up, tail wagging in greeting. She gobbles down half a bowl of chicken-flavored kibble, has a short walk with Tina and Kim, and is by the door when the van motor revs, ready to jump up onto the front seat for the drive to work.

At 8:00 A.M., the van pulls up at the tidy industrial-park offices of Fahey Pest Control, Inc. Snooper hops out and passes the blasé office workers at Luxury Lighting, who are no longer surprised at seeing a dog going to work. She leads Kim up the grass-lined walkway and through the front door, just another regular employee on the nine-to-five grind.

Coworkers stop by Kim and Snooper's office, cheered by the familiar sight of their company dog. "Hey, Snoop," they tease, "gonna find us some ter-mites today?" Snooper thumps her tail, reacting to the friendly voices and smiling faces, but not to the word "termites." She's been trained only to rec-ognize the code letter T, to prevent her from entering search mode whenever she hears "termites" around the office or on the job.

Out of the office and into the van, Snooper's tail signals her pleasure, knowing the first job is coming up. A few miles later, she is inside a big house, smelling the Christie family's burning toast, bombarded by the sounds of eight boisterous children. She pulls on the leash as Kim removes the small plastic pill bottle from her apron pocket and explains to the children that the live termites within will give Snooper something to find, a reward if the house has no pests. The bottled bugs also test the dog's alertness and help make sure she is geared up for the hunt.

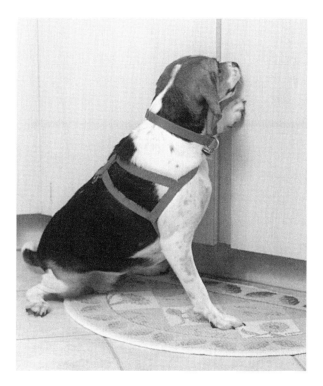

Kim hides the bottle and returns to find Snooper captivated by the children's affection, distracted by the bacon smells, and disoriented by the air-conditioning, which the office had instructed the Christies to turn off. Retreating to the relative quiet of the upstairs master bedroom, Kim taps her pointer and commands, "Find the Ts," Snooper's signal to start the search. Snooper tugs on the leash, sniffing diligently around the baseboard, so focused Kim knows she's in the zone.

All clear, except for the planted termites Snooper finds in the pill bottle under the bed.

"Good girl," Kim encourages, scratching and kissing her dog, pleased Snooper found the plant, assured she's turned on.

On the landing, followed closely by eight pairs of tiny feet, Kim taps and Snooper goes to work, sniffing the juncture of the walls and floors in the bathrooms, bedrooms, kitchen, dining room, basement, and all three floors of the large Christie residence. Snooper can't see the secretive insects that live in narrow cracks and crevices, avoiding bright light. She works solely by scent, tracking an amazing conglomeration of termite odors, including pheromones, chemical trails left by the termites as they seek new food sources, and the smell of microbial digestion produced by symbiotic microorganisms that shelter and feed inside the termite gut, aiding the termite in breaking down and digesting tough wood fibers.

Suddenly, Snooper stops, the two hundred million olfactory cells in her super nose zooming in on one particular smell. Decisively, she taps the wall three times with her front paw. Of the forty-five different termite species in the U.S., causing more than 1.5 billion dollars in damage per year, Snooper has detected the nests of *Reticulitermes flavipes*, the Eastern subterranean termite, a tough foe. Excitedly, Kim recognizes that her efficient, well-trained, slow-to-rise beagle has given her first clear alert of the day.

· · ·

As a six-month-old puppy, Snooper was flown to Maryland by her termite control company to train with the dean of termite beagle trainers, Dr. Andrew Solarz. Spurred on by her curious, exploratory nature in a three-month, twelve-step, $7,000 training program, Snooper learned the tricks of her trade. She achieved a high level of obedience, learned to maneuver through small, tight spaces, respond to thirty-five voice commands, and, most important, recognize the smells of the different termite species as well as other noxious insects like carpenter ants. Underscoring the gentle, positive training was Snooper's innate desire to please her handler. Without her strong work ethic, no training method would have succeeded.

Snooper earned her Beacon Termite Detection Canine Certificate by correctly alerting to fifty consecutive termite-infested sites. Her framed graduation certificate hangs in the office, a reassuring guarantee that, for $190, Snooper can locate wood-munching pests with an accuracy greater than ninety-eight percent.

Now, Snooper is an ace termite finder, better than any machine. In 1996, at a Pennsylvania entomology conference, a beagle took on the newest mechanical termite-divining device and a high-tech fiber-optic detector. The dog blew both machines away. The final termite-colony detection score: beagle, 12; machines, 2.

Snooper's on a tight schedule, and the team heads off to check a termite-control system installed three weeks earlier. Snooper hops out of the van and trots into the familiar house, eagerly tracking along baseboards, inside cupboards, and through the basement, remembering the rooms where she located termite infestations a few weeks before. This time, no termites, only the planted buggy pill bottle, some beef-flavored kibble, and a scratch with a kiss, rewards as fine as if she had found rampant colonies of termites devouring the walls.

Next stop is the Glens' retirement dream home, a quick, efficient clearing operation for a termite dog. Kim points and Snooper sniffs, Kim helping Snooper around obstacles, both ends of the leash working in tandem.

"Are there Ts here?" Kim asks, continually surprised that any dog, even one with as sensitive a nose as a beagle, can detect the scent of such well-hidden bugs. Snooper stops and scratches at the wall with nails that have been neatly trimmed, so she doesn't damage the paint. Kim marks the spot with a piece of tape and rewards Snooper with beef kibble, an on-the-job treat different from her at-home chicken-flavored fare.

"Good girl!" she enthuses, as Snooper gulps down her treat and tugs lightly on her leash.

"More?" Kim asks. "More Ts?"

Snooper aims her nose toward the juncture of wall and floor, along the baseboard in the kitchen, through the dining room, three bedrooms, first floor, second floor, down into the basement. Eleven times, Snooper stops in mid-stride, pasting her nose to the wall or floor for a closer sniff, signaling three times with her paw.

The retired couple had tried numerous frustrating inspection services, who drilled holes, made messes, set traps, and visually checked for termites, all to no avail. The unresolved problem gnawed at their sense of security.

With her search completed, Snooper has sniffed out the problem, uncovering eleven active termite colonies inside the couple's walls and floors. If left unchecked, the bugs could soon number in the millions, and carry immense potential for damage—as few as sixty thousand termites can consume a one-foot length of two-by-four-inch pine in 125 days.

Mission accomplished, the hardworking beagle jumps back into the van, leaving the Glens to implement the termite-control program in the specific sites she has identified. Thanks to her, the relieved couple can finally enjoy a worry-free retirement. But for Snooper, it's all in a day's work, and there's one last stop before quitting time.

She stays alert as the van weaves through traffic, but Kim can tell from her furrowed brow that the heat and intense work are taking their toll. Perhaps because it's Friday, perhaps because the warm July weather makes the Florida termite population especially ravenous, Snooper has had a busy day.

"Almost done," Kim promises affectionately, patting her partner. As if she can read her handler's mind, Snooper sits up, tail erect and wagging.

It's almost 5:00 P.M. when they reach the old Miller estate at the edge of town. Dispensing with preliminaries, Kim urges, "Find the Ts." The beagle pads through the living room sniffing the edges of the carpet, stops, paws at the floor in the well-worn ritual, and receives her reward. On the way back to the van after the last service call of the week, Snooper exhales a long, exhausted sigh.

At home, Snooper wolfs down a well-earned bowl of chicken-flavored kibble, laps up her cool water, and sits quietly while Kim brushes out her shiny coat and trims her nails. Snooper's grooming finished, Tina, the pet beagle, approaches, prancing teasingly in front of her friend, hoping to entice her to play. But the hardworking canine doesn't even notice her. Snooper is already fast asleep on the living-room rug, dreaming of the boating weekend ahead, her long ears twitching slightly in an imaginary breeze.

CONNECTICUT, U.S.A.

BRUNO

Bruno's chameleon face perks up like a pet dog with a Frisbee. When the seven-year-old German shepherd is buckled into his harness and hooked to the fifteen-foot tracking leash, he knows his work is about to begin. While Bruno's busy being outfitted, the waiting suspect seizes the opportunity to escape, scuffing the ground with his shoe as he tears down the street, clutching a big branch.

Quickly, Bruno's handler, patrolman Bill Proulx, leads him to the fresh scuff marks, lets him sniff, and sets him on the suspect's trail. Nose to the ground, pausing only once to correct his heading, Bruno powers forward, pulling his partner behind. Straight, strong, intense, he doesn't hesitate.

Three hundred yards down the asphalt, directly in front of the suspect's hideaway, he stops. A hundred pounds of coiled muscle holds the suspect at bay.

"Whatagoodboy, whatagoodboy!" Proulx praises his dog in a high-pitched, affectionate falsetto, more concerned about an encouraging tone for his dog than the loss of his macho baritone.

Smiling, the fake suspect, a fellow police officer, hands over the hunk of tree—Bruno's reward.

"Careful with that stick," jokes Proulx, "it's Bruno's favorite. He's had it over a year."

Bruno scampers around Proulx all the way to the car, urging him in a singsong play-bark—half howl, half woof—to throw the stick again and again. He retrieves it, then hangs on tightly, as he was taught, biting and tugging it away from Proulx with his powerful jaws. He doesn't let go until Patrolman Proulx of the East Hartford, Connecticut, police department commands, "Break," a chilling reminder of what this exuberant dog's play is all about.

Bruno is a graduate of the elite Connecticut State Police Canine Training Unit, one of the oldest police dog academies in North America. Each year, twenty aspiring police dogs enter, but only five graduate. Bruno cut his teeth at this doggie boot camp, and returns regularly to keep in shape, climbing ten-foot-high hurdles, tunneling through long passages, clambering up and down metal ladders, leaping through hanging tires, and scaling piles of stacked barrels. Fine breeding, keen intelligence, and top-notch training make Bruno an ace athlete and problem solver. His success rate at locating suspects is twice the national average for tracking dogs. He's found nine lost kids, three of whom no one else could track. And he's assisted and protected his partner, Bill Proulx, on eight hundred arrests, half involving dangerous felons. Proulx says that even checking building alarms can be dangerous. "Bruno goes in alone, and if he locates the suspect, he bites and holds him. There are lots of cases in the United States in which policemen have been shot checking out an alarm. Bruno takes the brunt of the danger; he goes through the door first."

For relaxation, Bruno and Proulx compete in the Connecticut K-9 Olympics, a closely judged series of obstacle courses, searching tests, and police skills events, which they have won twice.

Bruno comes by his skills naturally. Strong, aggressive, and motivated, yet tractable, intelligent, and friendly, he combines the best of his breed's desirable police dog qualities. Versatile German shepherds were first standardized as herding and guarding dogs in the 1890s by Captain Max von Stephanitz, and have since excelled in a variety of careers, from military work to guiding the blind. Ever since the first police dog academy was established in Ghent, Belgium, in 1899, male German shepherds have been the dogs of choice for police work.

Initially, Bruno was bred as a guide dog. Raised by a foster family for the first year of his life, he was judged unsuitable for guiding because he chased squirrels and was shy about loud noises. He was assigned to Proulx at eighteen months old, graduated top dog in the police academy, and started working the streets when he was two years old. Proulx acclimatized his gun-shy dog to noise by spending months at the shooting range during his lunch hour, gradually exposing him to louder and louder gunfire. As for Bruno's fondness for chasing, in his new job, that isn't a problem.

The Night Shift

Three-thirty P.M.
Bruno and Proulx pile out of their plain white Ford and head downstairs to the lineup room for the night shift's briefing. The big shepherd flops on his side on the concrete floor while the supervisors instruct the patrolmen, many of whom stoop to pat Bruno's head and ruffle his fur. At schools, Cub Scout

meetings, and on the street, hands are always reaching out to touch him. When he is surrounded by strangers, Bruno's eyebrows rise quizzically. He endures, face stoic and resigned. But in the station house among friends, he gladly accepts the caresses, a model of dignity and reserve.

Bruno waits patiently, but as soon as Proulx signals, he bounds outside, prancing around his partner in anticipation, "dancing by the car ready to jump in when he knows it's the real thing. He wants to go to work. He's a motivated employee."

Four P.M.

Beat number twenty, the toughest beat in downtown East Hartford.

Bruno and Proulx, back in the white Ford, cruise the main street until they see a motorist run a red light. Pulling him over, they slip into their well-oiled routine.

Bruno hangs half out the window, three paws on the windowsill, one back leg hooked inside the car, barking and growling, putting the fear of dog in the driver. A strip of traction tape along the top edge of the window secures his footing. If he were to slip, it would not only ruin the paint, but also destroy his spectacular intimidation posture.

Proulx approaches the vehicle warily. He is thinking about another night just like this, when a speeding car almost sideswiped his cruiser and the K-9 team went after it. Proulx pulled the speeder over on an entry ramp of the highway, and discovered that the car was stolen. He approached the car, asking the driver to step out of the vehicle, "and instead of stepping out, he started the car up. I grabbed for the keys, and he put the vehicle in drive and took off on the ramp of this highway, dragging me for a good distance. I didn't call for Bruno to help me because I was afraid he'd be run over, but after I was dragged a few seconds I realized that Bruno was in the suspect's car and, uh, Bruno was biting the suspect's right arm."

That memorable night, Bruno's quick action, total devotion, and excellent training saved Proulx's life. On another occasion, Bruno did it again. "Shots were going off, a man was running straight at me pointing a gun, and I forgot I even had a dog. I just started firing at him, trying to stop him before he could shoot me, and I guess I dropped the leash. Bruno knew what to do. On his own initiative, he went after the person, took him right off his feet. I trust his judgment." Bruno's heroic actions earned him the state's highest life-saving award, and the trust between Bruno and Proulx, the vital bond between police dog and handler, was cemented forever.

Proulx stops beside the driver's door and asks for his registration.

Bruno barks and blusters in the background.

Proulx smiles affably as he writes the ticket.

The motorist accepts the ticket willingly, keeping a wary eye on Bruno.

Moments later, the good cop, "bad dog" are on their way.

Rush Hour

The routine repeats itself, through an expired registration, a broken window, a fleeing suspect, a sexual assault, and a domestic dispute that diffuses the moment they arrive. Mostly, Bruno is a friendly dog. Strangers can come up and pat him and kids can lie on him and pull his tail. But there's fire in him, and with voice and body language Proulx knows how to modulate Bruno's moods. "When we want the fire, we turn it on, like turning on a light switch. We turn it on and he'll be aggressive, we turn it off again and the dog is very calm and very laid-back."

The Post-rush Lull

Call by call, the early evening demand abates. To keep Bruno's morale up and compensate for the high percentage of tracking failures when suspects escape in cars, Proulx arranges for a little reinforcing fun.

They race into the parking lot of a closed car dealership, lots of space, very few people, police siren screaming—their second training exercise of the day.

A waiting police officer, playing "suspect," stands at the edge of a field of tall grass wearing a protective training sleeve.

Proulx, Bruno, and another K-9 team practice "hits," a pursuit-and-capture routine that is part of their daily training.

Proulx leaps from the car.

"Stop," he threatens, "or I'll release the dog."

The suspect runs a few steps along the pavement then plunges into the long grass and disappears.

"Get him," Proulx commands, and Bruno jumps from the car, locks onto the trail, flashes across the asphalt, and disappears into the long grass, Proulx running behind.

In a blink of an eye, Bruno bites and holds the fugitive.

In panic, the man begs to have the dog called off. Bruno clings like grim death to his arm. Proulx rushes in.

"Stand still," he orders, a command with a dual purpose. Most suspects think the words are for them and usually obey. Really, the instruction is for Bruno, preparing him to let go.

"Break," Proulx commands, and Bruno instantly releases the man's arm as if dropping his stick.

Then, surprisingly, Bruno wags his tail, panting happily. For him, training is a form of play. Proulx pats his back, rolls around on the ground with him, "getting down on the dog's level, getting in there and just playing with him like a little kid. You can't be afraid to do that." Bruno nudges his partner's hand, darts quick licks at his face.

Trained to be intimidating, Bruno looks like an uncontrollable, unstoppable force of nature when he attacks. Yet his chases, grabs, holds, and growls are predictable and conscious. When told to let go, he complies instantly. He switches off the fury and wags his tail.

Proulx cuddles Bruno and tosses his stick, counting on regular practice to keep Bruno's lifesaving skills sharp, knowing "things aren't this dramatic in real life, but the time you need it the dog has to do it right." Bruno revels in the attention, frisking around his partner, barking excitedly—his master's satisfaction his greatest reward.

Then, he settles down as Proulx puts leashes, harnesses, and his treasured stick into the trunk of the car along with a dog first-aid kit, a water dish, a change of clothes for Proulx, and the essential bottle of window cleaner and roll of paper towels to clean his persistent nose prints off the inside of the windshield.

Ten P.M.

Dispatch calls start piling up again. Drunk drivers are on the road, causing trouble. Bruno and Proulx make a couple of traffic stops and arrest a hit-and-run.

Twelve Midnight

Proulx gets an urgent call for the K-9 team to assist an officer in breaking up a knife fight. The white Ford accelerates and Bruno lifts his head from the backseat, where he's been napping. Whether by scent or sixth sense, Bruno knows his friend is on alert. He pops up and stares eagerly out the windshield, forepaws on the back of the front seat, tail wagging.

"Good boy," Proulx says, welcoming him.

Bruno wriggles with excitement. His master's tone and timbre confirm action ahead.

By the time Bruno and Proulx reach the scene, the combatants have been separated but one of the men is still yelling, incensed and incoherent. People are gathering, some loud and obviously intoxicated, a crowd drifting in the wrong direction.

Bruno and Proulx mingle with the angry crowd. During their three months of intensive training at the K-9 academy, Bruno learned to bark. He learned to bark a lot.

Stationed among the milling crowd, Bruno fires up and begins to yelp, bark, and grumble, vocalizing more and more aggressively. To outsiders, Proulx looks convincingly like a handler with a menacing animal barely under control.

People fall back, the tone of the crowd changes subtly. "He's great at keeping people back; nobody seems to want to test a police dog." Bruno is not only intimidating, he is also interesting. People are curious.

Now the K-9 team moves to a position at the edge of the action as other officers continue the negotiations. Bruno chimes in with a bark now and then but for the most part the team simply watches and waits.

Bruno observes Proulx closely, head raised, ears cocked, attuned to his partner's every sound and movement. Nothing gets by him. He is alert and aware, his quick intelligence processing the barrage of sensory information. He watches Proulx assessing the activity around them. When the suspect is about to be handcuffed, Proulx tenses. Bruno rises to his feet in response. It's always dangerous when an angry person has to accept restraints, the last chance to resist.

The suspect's eyes shift; he hesitates, staring at the handcuffs.

"Watch," Bruno hears, almost in a whisper, and the command triggers a ferocious round of barking.

Then, Bruno feels Proulx's subtle tug on his collar. Unlike a pet dog, Bruno has learned to lunge, not stop, in response to pressure on his collar.

Bruno launches himself toward the suspect, barking fiercely. Totally confident, free of the fear that accompanies normal aggression, without even baring his teeth, he looks frighteningly violent. The effect is dramatic.

Immediately, the suspect holds up his hands to be cuffed.

An officer snaps on the cuffs, Proulx signals, and Bruno quiets down. Now that his well-schooled capacity for violence is no longer needed, his calm, amiable nature resurfaces.

He wags his tail, pleased to be of service.

Proulx ushers the still agitated, cursing suspect into the front seat of his patrol car.

"Into the car," he orders Bruno.

The big German shepherd vaults easily through the driver's window, practically landing on the suspect's lap, then bounces into the backseat.

"The dog is behind you," warns Proulx, pointing out something the suspect already finds painfully obvious.

The man nods and stares straight ahead. He's not yet calm, but he is finally silent.

Proulx glances toward the backseat and hides a smile. Bruno the vicious police dog is curled up on the seat having another nap. Truth is, Proulx knows, Bruno likes visitors in his car and could wake up anytime and give the suspect a big, welcoming, not-so-reassuring lick. Proulx thinks, "I wouldn't want to do this job without my dog."

One A.M.

All quiet.

End of the night shift and the K-9 team heads home.

Proulx pets Bruno, as he often does during the long hours they spend driving around in the car together. "You have to spend a lot of time with the animal, taking him for walks, feeding him, petting him, praising him. You bond with your dog over time."

"Good boy, buddy, whatagoodboy, whatagoodboy," Proulx croons as they call it a night.

Home for Bruno is on fourteen acres of land in rural eastern Connecticut with Proulx, his wife, Amy, and their two young children, Ryan and Nicole. Quite often, people ask Proulx where Bruno lives, imagining he lives in a cage in the police station like a robot. "When Bruno isn't working, he comes home with me, and he's just a pet, a big baby, and he does what he wants." Mostly he hangs out where the action is, keeping underfoot. While Proulx sleeps, Bruno waits outside the bedroom door, where little Ryan used to lay his head on his furry side and sleep with him. Bruno also spends a lot of time playing with Dakota, Proulx's six-month-old German shepherd. Proulx likes Bruno to socialize with kids and other animals because at work he's often dealing with dangerous, violent people, "and you don't want him to think everyone's bad."

Bruno is already passing on his knowledge to Dakota, although the puppy will enter the academy only when he's about two years old. Gradually, by example and play, Bruno teaches him sociability, coordination, self-control, and tracking—skills that will ensure Dakota and Proulx's safety in the years to come. Then Dakota will take his place alongside patrolman Bill Proulx and Bruno can retire and stay home with the people he loves, surrounded by sugar bush and the fields he likes to roam. There is a river nearby, where he and Dakota frolic refreshingly. And because there are woodstoves in the house and a wood-fired evaporator in the sugar cabin, every year Proulx will cut Bruno thirty or forty cords of fetching sticks to play with, whenever he likes.

PART TWO

HERDING DOGS

· · · · · · ·

GLOUCESTERSHIRE, ENGLAND

SWEEP

Sweep lies immobile, ears flat, small black-and-white body pressed tightly into the green grass. He is so still, only his darting brown eyes reveal that he's thinking, watching, listening.

Suddenly, in response to a low voice command, he is in motion, streaking across the field, away from his master, Dick Roper. Sweep is now a mere speck on the horizon. Head low to the ground, almost crouching, hindquarters high, tail tucked between his legs, he arcs wide around the grazing sheep six hundred yards away.

A large dominant ewe sidles protectively toward her charges and turns to confront the rapidly approaching Border collie.

Circling closer to the flock, Sweep begins to narrow the distance between him and the sheep, eyeing them, willing them to obey, to follow his directions.

The battle-scarred ewe snorts her displeasure. Weighing twice as much as Sweep, she readies to assert her authority. She paws the ground furiously, points her imposing bulk at the young sheepdog, and holds her ground, the flock bunched behind her.

Sweep slows to a walk, eyes never leaving his adversary's face. He inches forward steadily.

The ewe prepares herself for the charge.

The crowd gasps.

Sweep's Border collie herding instinct is unequaled in the canine world. His inherited prowess, exceptional athletic ability, and responsive nature make his breed the top sheepherder known to mankind.

In the nineteenth century, hardworking sheepdogs were essential to the process of turning vast, unfenced Scottish and English borderlands into prime sheep-raising country. Urban growth from the Industrial Revolution created large markets for lamb, mutton, and wool. Ranchers had to manage large flocks of flighty sheep spread over inhospitable hillsides, and herd them for shearing, driving to market, and relocation from one field to another. To make their faithful farm collies even more useful for herding, shepherds began to crossbreed for helpful traits from other breeds, adding the controlling "eye" of the staunch setter and the speed and silent nature of the whippet, a sight hound. The resulting nineteenth-century collie-setter-whippet mix was the genesis of the modern Border collie, a medium-sized black-and-white dog renowned for its unusual combination of grace, agility, hardiness, and stamina.

Border collies are fanatically dedicated to herding sheep. They can distinguish slight variations among the many different whistles they understand and can respond appropriately to each one, from as far as a mile away. They instinctively fan out wide in order to gather large groups of sheep at one time, and creep up slowly in order not to spook the sheep and make them run. They use "eye," a threatening glare, to stare down and move the sheep, pushing them along by controlled intimidation. This technique is probably related to wolves' tactic of selecting a victim in the herd by catching its eye and asserting their dominance before starting the attack run.

Different breeds have different herding styles. Corgis dart in and nip. Big dogs like rottweilers and Bouviers are drovers, physically butting up against the stock to move them. But because Border collies' early work was to gather sheep from the hills, they are, by nature, gatherers rather than drovers. They are lightning fast, yet able to stop or switch directions in an instant.

Border collies are recognized in respected studies as the smartest dog breed in the world. Bred for two hundred years for their intelligence and herding skills, rather than their physical appearance, they have so far escaped many of the inbred genetic diseases affecting other purebred dogs. For this reason, they remain one of the few breeds still fulfilling a traditional role in their homeland.

An Eye for the Sheep

It's 5:00 A.M. and the only sign of life in the old stone farmhouse is a light in the kitchen visible from the hills above the valley. Inside, chilled from the outdoors, curled up and pretending to sleep, is Sweep. He huddles next to the old Aga stove, soaking in its warmth, one cocked ear listening to the cold wind outside, one eye watching Dick's every movement. Dick sits at the round wooden table. He sips a cup of coffee and chuckles to himself at the newspaper headline.

ROBOT DOG
SCIENTISTS DEVELOPING ROBOT SHEEPDOG

"It looks like you might be out of a job in a few years," he says to Sweep. "You better get your skates on." Sensing the moment he's been waiting for,

Sweep bounds up and sits taut as a coil by the door. Finally, Dick is ready and they head out to the truck to start the day.

Sweep's sire, now retired, and Dick's other Border collie bark and yelp excitedly as Sweep and Dick approach.

"Quiet, you'll wake the whole household," Dick warns, and the dogs fall silent.

Sweep is first to jump into the back of the truck, oblivious to the other dogs. His eyes are alert, raring to work. Sitting up, head high, he sees the narrow country road, the turnoff three miles down, then the dirt lane. Dick gets out to open the familiar gate, then, finally, they reach the last stop, a dry stone wall in the corner of the field. The grass is lush here, green and ready for nibbling.

Light breaks into the darkness as Sweep, trembling with excitement and readiness, leaps down from the back of the truck. In a distant pasture,

out of sight but carried by the wind, he hears the low bleating of awakening sheep.

"Away," Dick says softly.

Sweep shoots off across the field, curves around the flock of five hundred sheep, and waits at the rear of the herd.

"Stand," Dick yells across the field, and Sweep drops to the ground, eyes fixed on the moving sheep, perfectly still but for the twitch of his ears. Sweep hears the sound, barely discernible to the human ear, of Dick's whistle commanding his next move. Crouched, his forequarters lower than his haunches, he advances, never getting too close to the sheep. Deftly, he maneuvers the flock through wooden gates, over streams, and around ditches.

A small group of ewes and their lambs break from the main herd and bolt for the hilltop. Sweep reacts instantly, shooting off through the field out of Dick's sight. Craftily cutting off the errant sheep's escape route, he reappears like a missile zooming over the rolling countryside and turns the wayward sheep back toward the flock.

A disoriented lamb stands alone, calling plaintively for its mother.

Dick commands Sweep to "mother-up," pointing first to the lamb, then to a frantic ewe within the herd. Sweep obeys, rounding up the lost lamb and reuniting it with its mother.

Fast and silent, tracking back and forth on the edge of the flock, Sweep moves the sheep at a steady pace forward, toward his shepherd, Dick.

Sweep was brought to England from Ireland by a man transporting greyhounds. Exhausted by the long trip, the little thirteen-week-old puppy still managed to impress his new owner. Away from his mother and littermates for the first time, he sat confidently in the front passenger seat, paws on the dashboard, quietly watching the traffic all the way home to the farm. That first week, Dick remembers, young Sweep seemed manic. "I've never seen any-

thing like it. His instinct was to work anything that moved—the cat, dripping
water, sheep. I took him out with me in the truck on the second day. While
my other dogs were bringing in the sheep, Sweep squeezed out of a small side
window of the truck and tried to herd them, too."

The two other collies drove the sheep toward Dick and Sweep drove
them sideways, just for the sheer joy of herding.

It was chaos.

"It took ages to catch him. I realized this was a very, very unusual dog.
He is exceptionally bright, which can be difficult, but I knew if I could harness it, he would be brilliant."

Sweep's training began almost immediately. Dick emphasized repetition, clarity, and consistency, constantly giving verbal feedback to his new pup. By the tone of Dick's voice, Sweep learned "no" meant wrong and "good" meant correct. "The tone of the voice did it. I am his pack leader and he expects to be told when he is wrong and encouraged when he is right." Sweep's only punishment was banishment to the truck so that he couldn't work. "You can't have gray areas with a Border collie. Consistency is everything. They love it."

When Sweep was fifteen weeks old, Dick brought him to the fields for his first real herding assignment. The puppy took up his position behind the twenty ewes and drove them around at a beautiful pace, "never coming in and being 'dirty' or biting. He's a natural; his turns were natural, both flanking turns and turning out. He was positive; he would stand and 'square,' or look sheep head-on, which doesn't happen often. This was all natural to him." The hardest command for Sweep was to move the sheep away from his master; his herding instinct said bring them to the top dog, now firmly established as Dick.

By the age of seven months, Sweep was fully trained, and he and Dick had formed an inseparable bond.

The sun is high in the sky on the day of the Welsh National Sheepdog Trials. Sweep and Dick have traveled five hours along the highway and over rugged hills to windswept Aberystwyth, on the coast of Wales. Onlookers sit on blankets overlooking the fifty-acre field, or watch from their cars, their pent-up, twitchy pet Border collies eyeing the scene with interest. Sweep and Dick join fifty other sheepdog/shepherd teams, many of whom have traveled long distances with their families to attend and compete in this prestigious national trial.

As soon as their names are announced, Dick takes his place in the field beside the wooden starting marker, in front of the judge's tent. Sweep waits by his side, ears perked, body coiled, quivering for action.

A bell rings, signaling the start of the twenty-minute trial. Seven sheep, one large matriarch and six younger ewes, are released from a holding pen on the hillside six hundred yards away.

"Away," Dick commands, motioning to the right to signal the "outrun," a directed sprint to the livestock waiting on the hill. Sweep is eager and takes off in a flash, tearing across the main field in a wide right-hand arc toward the sheep. Born to herd, just as horses are born to run, Sweep embodies his heritage and training in his spare frame, the perfect physical herding machine. His slender limbs reach and fly, a dark blur against the green turf.

The moment Sweep reaches the herd, the big ewe turns to face him. Undaunted, Sweep creeps forward steadily. All his instincts tell him it's important to gain this dominant female's respect if he wants the other sheep to obey.

The ewe snorts, paws the ground, and butts her head in Sweep's direction, readying for the charge. The little Border collie glares back, unafraid, his hypnotic "eye" locked onto the ewe's face, seeking to mesmerize and control the unruly sheep.

The standoff lasts barely seconds.

The ewe is aggressive but also wise. She glances back at her flock and again at the singleminded sheepdog. Sensing Sweep's courage and iron determination, the old ewe turns briskly and rejoins her flock. Sweep moves in quickly. In full command again, he efficiently "fetches," or herds, the flock through a seven-yard-wide central gate toward Dick, now only one hundred and fifty yards away.

Standing at his post, eyes narrowed against the sun, Dick guides Sweep through the rest of the competition, the pitch of his voice controlling his dog's pace. The Border collie drives the sheep, unrushed and unafraid, across the long triangular field, "driving" them smoothly through more narrow gates to an enclosed ring. Here, Sweep has to separate out two reluctant, clannish sheep, "shedding" them from the herd.

Feinting left, then right, nipping and darting, always attentive to Dick's commands, the agile sheepdog neatly divides the flock.

Now Sweep must gather his flock together again and herd them into a small pen, the final and, often, the most difficult part of the trial. Time is crucial. Dick and Sweep have only five minutes left to complete the "penning" stage of the trial.

Fed up with being herded, the impatient sheep try to escape to the hillside to graze.

Dick watches, holding open the gate of the pen, not allowed to assist his dog in any way except with his voice. "Away," he commands, "Bye," "Stand," "Come," in rapid succession. Sweep responds, moving fluidly in and out of the flock, his sinewy body in constant motion, working the sheep back toward the pen.

Three sheep in, two more to go.

Sweep heads out to round up the last pair and the penned sheep make a run for freedom.

The crowd gasps.

Sweep stops, blocks their path, then turns on a dime and nimbly herds the last defiant couple into the pen.

Dick clangs the gate shut with only seconds to spare.

The crowd holds their breath, waiting for the final score.

"Number seventeen, Sweep, black-and-white rough-coated, two years six months, eighty-seven qualifying points—Position one! *We have a new champion!*" crackles the loudspeaker.

Cheers and applause ring out from the Welsh National Sheepdog Trials crowd, watching in admiration.

Dick calls Sweep to him, pats his haunch, and croons his warmest "good boy" reward. He marvels at Sweep's obedience and skills, never having known such a keen dog with such strong instinct.

Audience members rush across the field toward Dick and Sweep to congratulate them on their steady, elegant win. Only then does Dick relax, hugging Sweep to him, roughing up his head and back affectionately, making sure "the most intelligent and able Border collie I've known in all my twenty years" knows it's all over and he is pleased. Sweep's tongue lolls out of his mouth with exhaustion and his happy, panting face beams his contentment at a job well done.

Several shepherds approach Dick to book dates for breeding. Sweep excelled in his early trials and won four of the eight competitions he entered. Sheepdog enthusiasts recognize that Sweep has a future in international competition and they're banking on his future lineage.

Smoke curls from the chimney and a soft kitchen light illuminates the dark farmhouse. From his kennel in the converted stables, Sweep hears Dick clatter out the back door and across the cobbled courtyard toward him. He sits patiently, ears cocked, eyebrows twitching in stereo as Dick unlocks the door, fills his water bowl, and prepares his dinner. His glistening dark eyes never leave his master, even as he licks his bowl clean. As Dick leaves, Sweep jumps up, front paws against the wire of his door, wet black nose stuck as far as possible through the mesh, for one more glimpse of his shepherd.

"Good boy," Dick says in his soft voice.

Sweep sits back, satisfied and quiet. From the stalls beside him come the comforting sounds of his fellow sheepdogs settling in for the night. Soon it will be tomorrow, and he and Dick will be together again, working the sheep, doing what he's bred to do, what he loves best.

· · · · · · ·

KINGAROY, AUSTRALIA

BUSTER

Buster's forehead crinkles as he stares hard into the ferns and scrub surrounding the peppermint tree. An old cow lies straining on her side. She shudders, her four legs rising off the ground in a great effort to rid herself of some unseen burden. Buster watches anxiously as she bellows out her pain.

With Buster's attention distracted by the suffering cow, the other cattle stream around the tree, across the gully, and onto the other side of the creek. Buster hears Gary's trail bike buzzing up and down the far bank, trying to collect the errant cows and calves into one tight group. Still, Buster doesn't leave the laboring female. He edges forward and sniffs her hindquarters. Spotting a tiny protruding wet leg, Buster knows it's time to get help.

He takes off at a lope, but doesn't follow the creek like an inexperienced jackeroo on his first cattle drive. Instead, he seeks out the high ground running along the ridge to an old road he knows from chasing kangaroos, his favorite recreation. Silhouetted against the gray, overcast sky, Buster's strides eat up the ground. Within minutes, he spots the main herd below. Gary is charging back and forth like an angry bull as Taco, the rookie "doggeroo," struggles to help control the herd.

Buster heads off Gary's dusty bike, running alongside, then leading him back toward the creek and the stricken cow. Gary has no choice but to follow—he can't herd the cattle without Buster, and, besides, "Buster's my best mate, why would he lead me wrong?" Standing on the pedals to absorb the pounding shock, Gary follows his streaking Australian cattle dog across the rolling Queensland prairies.

At the top of the ridge, Buster disappears. Gary slams on the brakes and slides to a stop. Buster reemerges from the bushes, trots over to the bike, and lies down, looking at Gary as if to say, "I did my job, partner, now you do yours."

Parting the leafy tree fronds, Gary sees the birthing cow.

Buster's decision to suspend cattle driving and come to the aid of the endangered cow was guided by the complex mix of genes that constitute the Australian cattle dog. Ranchers developed this hardworking breed to move cattle efficiently across the wide open spaces of Australia's interior, where fences are scarce and ranch hands even scarcer.

Australian cattle dogs trace their roots back to the 1830s and a breed called the Smithfield, a sheepdog imported to Australia from England. The Smithfield had incredible stamina and could run all day, but its frequent barking caused the cattle to bolt and stampede. To overcome this drawback, an enterprising cattleman crossed the Smithfield with a hunting canine that never barked, the Australian wild dog, or dingo. The resulting dog controlled cattle silently by biting their hind legs, but was itself completely uncontrollable.

Ranchers then tried to mitigate the wildness of these "biters" by crossbreeding them with the smooth-coated Highland collie, a Scottish working dog with a distinctly colored blue merle coat. This mix produced an obedient dog that bit cattle on the heel on command. Unfortunately, the barking problem was back again. A third crossbreeding attempt added another dash of dingo, doubling the dingo dose to create the dog known as a Heeler. Heelers proved popular, but wreaked havoc during the cattle drives to market by insisting on herding the horses as well. Finally, two ingenious ranching brothers solved the conundrum by introducing dalmatian bloodlines, a breed known for its compatibility with horses and its work with horse-drawn fire wagons. The resulting offspring was then crossed with the kelpie, an Australian version of the Border collie. The final version of the Australian cattle dog was a red-speckled dog like Buster (or, in other cases, blue), half dingo, half combination of the other breeds. This canine composite possesses a reliable temperament and independent reasoning. Alert, quiet, strong, and tireless, the breed was accepted into the Australian Kennel Club in 1903.

Home on the Range

Buster opens one eye just before dawn. From the front porch, he sees the Southern Cross shining brilliantly above the horizon and pink fingers reaching up into the eastern sky. His ears tilt forward and through the screen door he hears the sizzle of two eggs plopping into a pan. The aroma of bacon curls around his nose.

Buster glances alertly toward the paddock. The fenced-in enclosure is empty, willowy peppermint trees waiting silently to shelter the shade-seeking Angus and Murray Grey cattle that will be brought home at the end of the day by seven-year-old Buster and his human companion, Gary. For three years, it's been just the two of them, with an occasional new pup, like the sixteen-month-old female, Taco, to train.

Buster knows the routine well. A big breakfast of bacon and eggs means a long, hard day driving cattle.

"Here, boy." The screen door swings open. "Did ya have a good night?"

Forty-two-year-old Gary Bazely places breakfast in front of Buster, scratches him between the ears, and unhooks his chain. Buster snaps up the small piece of steak that sits as a special treat on top of the dry food, and wags his tail hard, moist nose knocking bits of kibble onto the ground. He licks it all up and leaps down off the porch to join Gary. Before the tall, rangy cattleman can adjust his helmet and kick-start his trail bike, Buster has reached the creek, Taco close behind. They lap up the fresh flowing water, eyes glued to Gary.

The biking cowboy kicks his mechanical steed into gear and the two dogs explode out of the creek, spraying geysers of water. Forelegs fully extended, neck bobbing, and hind legs reaching ahead for maximum power, Buster runs beside Gary across the Australian plain. Taco slows to a trot, still developing her stamina, too young yet to maintain the ground-eating pace. Gary and Buster, cowboy and cowdog, speed over rolling hills through glens of flowering bramble, Buster agilely leaping the small water courses, Gary picking his way across the rocky bottomed, flowing streams. Together, they head to Gary's farthest pastureland, the "outback" of his 1,060-acre ranch.

An hour later, Buster and Gary reach their destination. From a hilltop overlooking the grazing field, they survey sixty of Gary's finest cows and calves—breeding stock and beef cattle ready for auction.

"Let's get 'em moving," Gary says. Buster needs no more encouragement. He heads off down a small coulee, staying hidden until he is on the far side of the cattle, trots right to pull in the herd, back left to tighten the flank, and moves in expertly from behind to push them forward. More than a hundred and fifty years of inventive selective breeding has created the perfect cowpoke on four legs. Gary watches his partner at work, always amazed that a dog with no formal training knows instinctively from an early age exactly what has to be done.

"One year old is a little late to break in a cattle dog," Kathe, a top breeder of Australian cattle dogs, told him, "but Buster is a good one." As a pup, Buster passed the broom test like a good heeler. "A good Australian cattle dog isn't scared of a charging eight-hundred-pound bull, so a broom's not going to faze them, even as a pup," Kathe explained. "Buster didn't only heel the broom, he also herded and nipped the seven other pups in his litter."

Gary took to the yearling from the moment he arrived, and the two quickly became great mates. To train him, all Gary had to do was be patient. Buster was a natural and caught on quickly.

Buster sweeps wide through the grass, stopping now and then to check the cows. Gary follows him down the hill, keeping his distance, holding back the newly arrived, panting Taco. Gary can see the dingo in Buster—the triangular, permanently erect ears, short muscular neck, bushy tail, and the stealth of his wild ancestors. Buster moves silently behind the cows. He stops, lowers his head slightly, and "eyes" three large dark Angus and a lighter Murray Grey. Responding to the glare of this tough little dog with its sharp teeth, the cows move briskly toward the cow path at the end of the pasture.

But two younger cows and a calf aren't yet ready to leave the dew-damp grass of the valley. They move languidly in the wrong direction, toward a brook at the pasture's edge.

"Go git 'em," Gary orders.

Wheeling about, Buster gallops to the right of the cows, his reddish coat blending into the brown grass along the side of the forest. He darts behind the largest straggler, crouches low, and with impeccable timing bites her right rear leg just as she steps down on it. Hopping onto her left leg, the cow lashes out with the right. But in the split second of her half step, Buster drops flat to the ground, and the cow's thrust cuts harmlessly through the air.

"He took a few to the head before learning cows are smarter than brooms," Gary remembers, thinking how keen his dog was, how quickly he caught on.

One more nip and the rogue cow trots to rejoin the herd. Buster takes a few steps toward the remaining two, and they quickly follow suit.

"Come behind," Gary calls, and Buster returns to the bike. Taco has succeeded in rounding up a few stragglers and the herd progresses up and over the hill. Now Gary works the lead, staying a little off to the side with Taco until they reach a shallow stream. Here, the herd splits, half fording the stream, half following the trail on Gary's side of the embankment.

"Git 'em, git 'em," Gary calls to Buster. "Git 'em NOW," he yells more urgently, knowing that upstream the water will be too deep to cross and collecting the herd again will be tough.

Buster has anticipated the danger. He moves quickly in a wide loop, coming around from downstream and cutting off the oncoming cows. He stops short to give them ample space to turn around, then rushes in with a few fake lunges. The cows splash back across the shallow part of the stream. Gary is ahead, out of sight with the first group, so Buster works the breakaway cattle from behind. When they stop to munch grass, he stops too. Only when they deviate from the path home does he move in and turn them, nipping and ducking to the ground when gentler methods fail. He catches up to Gary at a small pond. His thirty head join Gary's and the sixty cattle drink their fill.

"Go, boy, go, girl," Gary says encouragingly. Without hesitation, his two dusty dogs wade happily among the cattle for watery relief.

The sun arcs high in the sky, signaling the temperature has climbed to over a hundred degrees.

"Get 'em up, put 'em up," Gary urges, aware of the paucity of shade between the pond and the paddock. The dogs fan out to either side of the pond. Buster shows "eye," body flexed and ready to dash in if his authority is challenged. The cattle begin to move out, the whole herd soon back in motion. Gary is on his bike, Taco close by, Buster in the rear, moving the stragglers. Moving cattle is a two- to three-man job, but in ranch country outside Kingaroy, hands are scarce.

"Don't know what I'd do without Buster." Gary smiles to himself, watching his dog on the far side of the creek bringing in the last of the cattle. "He works harder than two hands and eats a lot less."

Gary turns the lead cows down the side path toward the ranch, Taco on guard at the fork. Despite her valiant efforts, half the cows forge straight ahead into the green grass beyond.

"Git 'em, git 'em," Gary calls to Buster.

But Buster is nowhere to be seen.

Gary speeds off to forestall the wandering cattle, leaving Taco to do the best she can at the turn.

"It's unlike Buster to abandon his post," Gary worries, feeling the strangeness of being on the plains without his dog. Buster is always with him—whether trotting along on the drive, lying close by at night, sitting by the bike, guarding the "ute," or utility truck, chasing the departing vehicle until it moves out of sight, or waiting on the porch of the farmhouse until he spies the telltale dust of Gary's return. All this flashes through Gary's mind as he scours the horizon for Buster and scrambles to collect the rapidly dispersing herd.

Buster reappears, running hard, without thought for the cattle spread out like water from a broken dam. Angling his body beside the dirt bike, he cuts Gary off, then leads him urgently along the beaten "'roo" track used by kangaroos. Overhanging ferns slap the cattleman's helmet, but the route brings them quickly to the stricken cow. Rolling up his sleeves, Gary gets down on his knees and braces himself, one hand on the cow's rump, the other firmly grasping the calf's slippery protruding hind leg. It's a breech birth and the calf is dangerously positioned, one hind leg trapped inside. If

Gary doesn't get it out soon, the calf will die from lack of oxygen. Gary pushes the little leg back into the cow's pelvic opening to give himself room to maneuver, and rotates the calf into position with a half twist. Close behind, Buster watches his master grasp both the calf's hind legs, and pull gently in time to the laboring cow's contractions. Two minutes later, the sticky, wet newborn slides out onto the ground. Gary quickly clears the mucus plugs from its small nostrils and vigorously rubs its sides to stimulate its breathing. Excited, Buster noses his way in and gives the bleating calf a helpful nudge. Taking Buster's hint, the exhausted mother cow struggles to her feet and begins licking and cleaning her baby.

"Atta boy, Buster!" Buster's tail thumps happily. "Good boy." Gary knows that without Buster both cow and calf would be dead. He grabs his dog around the neck, shaking his big, broad head. Buster licks his master's face. Gary looks back toward the bush, then to Buster, who has once more fulfilled his breed standard's promise of a dog that is "courageous and trustworthy, with an implicit devotion to duty."

"Let's go get 'em," he says, and Buster is off. The herd's stolen pasture holiday comes to an abrupt end. It's late afternoon, the clouds have broken up, and the cattle are back on the dirt track home. The sun is sinking behind the tall green mountains of the Great Dividing Range, shooting golden spires into the sky. Buster, Gary, and Taco spot the farmhouse on the rise.

"Put 'em up," Gary calls, and Buster quickens his pace. Gary speeds ahead and opens the gate, waving his hat at the cows as they flood into the paddock. Buster pushes the last one in. "He hates stragglers," Gary thinks, and closes the gate.

Gary beats the dust off his pants as he walks beside Buster up to the house. He can almost taste the cold Foster's, almost smell the steak on the barbie. This is his favorite time of the day and Buster's, too, but not for relaxing. The cattle driving over, Buster wants some good ol' cowpoke fun. Gary's hand reaches out to scratch Buster's head, but touches air. He turns to see Buster, a dusty ball shooting toward the pasture, where six silvery kangaroos are enjoying an evening nibble. The dog slices through the middle of the pack and shoots out the other side, turning and simultaneously trying to pick up speed. He heads for one kangaroo, veers off to another, pushing half the 'roos into the shelter of the trees, the other half left milling in the field. Gary laughs, seeing his dog torn between his two ancestral instincts: herding and chasing. In a last sprint, Buster chases the remaining 'roos into the woods, turns, and trots contentedly toward home, finally ready to call it a full wrangling day.

PART THREE

PERFORMANCE DOGS

· · · · · · ·

WOLF

Wolf doesn't even raise his head at the chorus of woofing and yapping next door in the backstage waiting area. Someone has let a beach ball loose and the other dogs in the Superdogs show are playing a wild, every-dog-for-himself rugby game. Wolf, the silky-coated borzoi, remains stretched out on the couch in the show manager's office in Montreal's Molson Center, his head tucked between his forepaws. He is the world champion canine high jumper, the marquee performer, and he is treated as such. He shares his private quarters only with Luna, his consort, who lies on the floor beside him. While the dog owners fall over one another trying to restore order in the sixteen-dog scrum next door, Wolf rolls onto his side and drifts back off to sleep.

At five years old, Wolf is already a four-year veteran of the Superdogs show. He is not only a world champion high jumper, but also a national obedience champion. This is a special feat, since borzois, also called Russian wolfhounds, are notoriously difficult to train. Both Wolf's world-record jumps and his obedience training are a testament to the skill and enormous patience of Seanna O'Neill, his owner and trainer.

In many ways, Wolf is the classic borzoi, an aristocratic dog of an aristocratic breed, with a few peculiar personality traits of his own. The borzois were bred by Russian nobility as elite wolf-hunting dogs in the fifteenth century. Their long, soft coats can be any combination of black, brown, gray, and white, and their slender frames and snouts are similar to those of greyhounds.

And, like greyhounds, they can run like the wind.

Wolf's borzoi ancestors reached the height of their popularity in nineteenth-century Russia, when nobles kept hundreds of borzois in palatial kennels, pampered between hunts by a small army of attendants and caretakers. In 1917, at the start of the Russian Revolution, the borzois became unwitting pawns on the losing side. Peasants storming country palaces slaughtered hundreds of them because they symbolized upper-class decadence.

The first borzois arrived in North America in the 1890s, but they are still rare, with less than 1,500 on the whole continent. And even borzoi fanciers warn that they are not for everyone. The Borzoi Club of America's list of people "Who Should Not Own This Breed" includes "people who think they don't need a fence because they have acreage in the country," "people without fences who live next to flocks of sheep and other valuable livestock," and "people who expect a high degree of instant obedience out of a dog." They add that borzois are not trustworthy off the lead and that most obedience-titled borzois are the product of long hours of training by skilled owners and handlers.

A Leap of Faith

Order restored backstage, tall, slender Seanna O'Neill and her oldest daughter check on Wolf and his companion, Luna. They are greeted by the thump-

thump of wagging tails. Slowly, Wolf eases off the couch and ambles over to Seanna, ears back, head slightly bowed in greeting. He looks at her adoringly as she leans down and strokes his neck. Seanna returns Wolf's affectionate gaze, remembering how challenging his training had been. An experienced trainer with four other dogs, Seanna learned that for training borzois, more than for most other breeds, she needed to develop insight into how her young pupil viewed the world. "You don't train a borzoi, you train with them," she discovered.

The Star Wars theme for the opening act of Hollywoof, the latest Techni-Cal Superdogs show, blasts through the arena sound system and Seanna ties a colorful bandanna around Wolf's neck. Superdogs is the largest, most popular dog show in history, playing to enthusiastic audiences around the world. Its founder, Herb Williams, compares Superdogs, with its costumes and choreo-graphed story lines, to a canine Cirque du Soleil, in which dogs perform humorous and athletic feats, along with running, jumping, and catching. The goal, Herb says, is to celebrate dogs for their heart and soul, as well as for their speed and agility.

Bubba, an Old English sheepdog sporting a Superdogs cape, bounds into the arena to the cheers of the crowd. In the opening act, Windows 2000, dogs fly through a series of colorful window-shaped hurdles, trying to beat the time set by a young boy called down from the audience. Bubba finishes with the fastest time, but the prized Superdogs cape is awarded to the boy. The crowd applauds its approval.

Hiccup, a little speed demon of a Yorkshire terrier, darts into the arena, jumping in the air, spinning, twirling, yapping, and generally showing off. He is chased by his frantic owner, who shouts commands, which Hiccup responds to on cue by doing the exact opposite. The crowd roars at the joke. These enthusiastic dog entertainers get pumped up for the performance as soon as the introductory music begins to play.

Wolf, on the other hand, remains perfectly calm while Seanna leads him to the waiting area. He seems almost oblivious to the choreographed commotion of Planet Venus, a game of doggie musical chairs, using large circular rubber mats instead of chairs. The music stops and the dogs scramble to appropriate one of the empty mats. Three- or four-way games of tug-of-war break out, and it soon becomes clear that Tadpole, the French bulldog, only takes part so he can joyfully demolish every mat he can sink his teeth into.

Wolf stands calmly behind the backstage curtain, ignoring the antics in the arena. He looks up at Seanna with a "ready any time you are" gaze. Wolf reminds Seanna of Duchess, his dam, a beloved companion and friend. She had not only been a champion in her own right, but the focus of much of Seanna's family life. Enrolled in Canadian Kennel Club obedience training since puppyhood, Duchess became not only the number one borzoi in obedience in Canada, but, in 1994, she was the number one dog in the hound group. Seanna's second borzoi, Icy, reached the level of number two hound, just behind Duchess. In the dog obedience world, it was almost unthinkable that two borzois were the top two hounds.

When she, Duchess, and Icy weren't at obedience trials, or playing flyball, an action-packed game involving catching balls and jumping hurdles, Seanna, a single mother in her mid-thirties, put on local action-packed dog shows, discovering that others were also delighted by the unbounded joy of her dogs at play. Seanna also wrote Superdogs manager Herb Williams describing her dogs' talents, then forgot about it. She was preoccupied that winter with Duchess, who was having puppies.

The pups were born in late January of 1994. There were nine in the litter, and eight of them were typical young borzois, spending virtually all their waking moments running, rolling, jumping, playing, and nipping. The ninth was Wolf. Even as a puppy, he was quiet and reserved. He watched the others with mild interest, then withdrew, alone, to snooze. That's why Seanna chose to

keep him. She was already busy with training and competitions for Duchess and Icy, and had just moved her family from Saskatchewan to Alberta in order to study Web page design. Wolf seemed a stay-at-home, don't-worry-about-me kind of dog. It was a good thing too, because that summer, life got even busier. Herb Williams called Seanna, inviting her to immediately join the Superdogs show then touring in Phoenix.

Within months of the Phoenix show, a terrible accident occurred that changed Seanna's and Wolf's lives. It was a summer afternoon, and somehow her three borzois, Duchess, Icy, and Wolf, managed to pry off a slat in Seanna's six-foot-high fence. They slipped through, sauntered off to see the world, and were soon doing what borzois love to do: chase things. Something caught their attention on the other side of the road, a squirrel perhaps, and all three tore off after it. Within seconds the three dogs were then struck by a passing car. Duchess and Icy were killed instantly, and young Wolf, less than a year old, was seriously injured.

Seanna was devastated by the loss of Duchess and Icy. But, in a way, it was their sudden deaths that gave Seanna a glimpse into the complex and wondrous world of Wolf. Looking back, Seanna says her reaction to the loss of her two dogs—and to Wolf, the survivor—was strange. Their deaths hit her harder than she realized, and Wolf, unobtrusive, seemed like part of the furniture. She ignored him for months, until one evening, when she was sitting in an easy chair in the living room, Wolf slid off the couch, approached her gently, and lay his head in her lap. He looked up with his deeply expressive brown eyes as if to say: They're gone, but I'm here. It's time to get on with it.

It was a poignant moment. Seanna realized she had been neglecting Wolf, and it was time at last to set aside her grief over Duchess and Icy. She began to pay more attention to Wolf, and what she discovered was a dog with superior intelligence, even for a borzoi, who seemed, almost in a human way, to know his own mind.

Both these qualities posed special problems for Wolf's training. In obedience training, dogs are supposed to do what they are told and not, as Wolf often did, decide for themselves if the command is truly necessary. Wolf didn't like to rise from a lying-down position. When he saw Seanna's hand signal to sit, even from across the yard, Wolf always sat. When he saw her hand signal to lie down, Wolf, with his typical grace, obeyed. But when he was commanded to sit up once again, he looked at Seanna quizzically. Hadn't she just told him to lie down? Wolf figured out that if he stayed down long enough, the dull training session, with its repetitive commands, would be over. While Seanna signaled and commanded, Wolf regarded her sympathetically, as if she were somehow confused. He remained comfortably stretched out on the soft carpet of the lawn.

Inside the house, Wolf learned how to deal with another irritant, Ferrari, Seanna's Jack Russell terrier. For some reason, Ferrari mercilessly tormented Wolf, yapping at him and nipping at his muzzle. Wolf waited until he and Ferrari were alone in the yard. Ferrari launched another assault. This time, Wolf was ready. In one swift motion, he scooped the small dog up with his mouth and tossed him six feet away. Ferrari didn't have a mark on him, but, for a time at least, he let Wolf be. Later, when Ferrari renewed his unprovoked attacks, Wolf repeated the move and it became a household ritual. Ferrari attacks, Wolf tosses him.

Eventually, by watching him closely, Seanna learned the training secret for Wolf. Don't give him time to think. From then on, Wolf moved through his training at an accelerated rate, exercising his quick intelligence without having time to ponder what he had learned. He made it through obedience training to become champion, completing all three Canadian Kennel Club levels in record time. With his natural athleticism, he also became a superb flyball player. But only on his terms. Now, during all-day tournaments, Wolf delightedly throws himself into morning games, but after a few hours he gets bored and wanders off, while other dogs race, hurdle, and catch balls all day long.

In jumping, Wolf found the sport he loves best. He was a natural, even as a pup, clearing flyball hurdles with almost ridiculous ease. Curiosity more than anything else led Seanna to test how high he could go. She was careful only to raise the bar in stages, and Wolf astounded her as he gradually jumped higher than any dog in the world had ever jumped. In 1998, at the Klondike Days Superdogs show in his home town of Edmonton, Wolf officially set the new world record at 62.5 inches. His feat was entered into the *Guinness Book of World Records*.

A change of music at the Molson Center signals the Superdogs jumping event. Wolf tenses, showing the first signs of excitement. But he has to wait for the right moment to make his entrance. Three jumps have been set up in the arena, taking up the length of the stadium. Each jump is progressively higher than the preceding one, and the last is double the height of the first. The competition among the other dogs begins. When each has made it over, the bars are raised. In between, the crowd roars as Hiccup shoots under the jumps, and Theodore, the Saint Bernard, crashes through them.

The bars are continually raised until all the dogs are progressively eliminated. Tension mounts in the arena. When it looks like the bars have reached an impossible height, a dramatic drumroll introduces Wolf. He saunters to the end of the arena. The crowd cheers. Wolf, energized now, trots to the starting point.

Even the wild and unpredictable crowd at the Superdogs show grows quiet. The comedy portion is over. The thirty-inch-tall borzoi sits quietly at Seanna O'Neill's side in front of the three jumps, the last one towering more than five feet high. The lights dim. Wolf glances up at Seanna. "You can do this," she says softly, encouragingly, and once again Wolf's ears tilt back at the sound of her voice. Seanna hopes he can't hear her heart pounding. She never looks at the final high bar because, even to her, it seems impossibly high for Wolf to clear.

Wolf doesn't look at the jump, either. He keeps his eyes on Seanna. He takes jumping seriously and has never refused to try a jump that Seanna requests.

If she says he can clear it, he no longer has any doubt.

He swings around, trots to the first jump, and hops over it. He moves slowly to the second, gathers speed at the last moment, and easily makes the jump. Then he jogs toward the third. It's higher than any dog in the world has ever jumped except him. He picks up speed and, at the last moment, like a rocket firing its afterburners, he is launched. With his paws in a perfect tuck, he leaps over the bar placed at more than twice his own height, clearing it with inches to spare. The crowd goes wild. Wolf, the world champion high jumper, prances around the arena like an Olympic athlete who has just won the gold. Then he bounds to Seanna for congratulations. For a moment, the quiet, reserved Wolf becomes an ebullient champion. His sudden burst of joy is infectious. "Wolf, Wolf, Wolf!" the crowd chants as Seanna hugs him.

After the show, the Superdogs are available for "paw-o-graphs." Thrilled by the show and smitten by the performers, kids crowd around to pat the dogs and receive stamped impressions of their paw prints. The two most popular paw-o-graph dogs are Hiccup and Wolf. Hiccup is ecstatic with the attention and jumps up and down, licking the faces of the children who come to pat him. But Wolf has by now recaptured his reserve. He allows his head to be stroked, but remains quiet, always keeping Seanna in view, waiting for her cue that it's a wrap.

Once touring is over, Wolf returns home to his normal routine. It includes brief daily training sessions, flyball tournaments, affectionate moments with Seanna, and the occasional Ferrari-tossing episode. Mainly it involves long hours sprawled contentedly on the living-room couch, Luna at his side. The next time Luna is in heat, Seanna intends to breed her with Wolf. She will be on the lookout for any pups who show the gentleness, self-confidence, and contentment with life that make Wolf a world champion and her special friend.

She is also looking again at Wolf's world record. The official results from Montreal prove Wolf actually jumped close to sixty-five inches, and she considers raising the bar next time to give Wolf the challenge he so enjoys. But she will be careful to make sure he is ready. With each jump Wolf takes, Seanna worries he will misstep and hit a bar. Not because he would hurt himself, the bars are light and come off easily. But simply because Wolf, after all they have been through together, trusts her not to ask more from him than he can give.

· · · · · · · ·

QUEBEC, CANADA

HAPPY RALPH

Happy Ralph, coal black, is first into the starting gate. He is sporting the number three. Seven other dogs are led into the narrow gate and final bets are placed. The mood is electric. Happy Ralph stands ready, every muscle clenched for an explosive start. The gun blasts, the gate opens, the mechanical rabbit is launched, and Happy Ralph leaps forward, first out of the gate.

In a dozen strides, he approaches forty miles per hour, the pack behind him, nothing but air between him and the speeding lure. In the stands, the smart money of the veteran gamblers is on Happy Ralph, and they urge him on, shouting, "Three! Three! Three!"

Lost in the moment of his great exertion, oblivious to the crowd in the stands, Happy Ralph rounds the final turn, the pounding legs and labored breathing of his competitors fading into the distance. He moves with the power and grace of a creature born to run. In Happy Ralph's case, he was also born to the track.

Since his birth in a greyhound puppy mill two years before, racing has been the sole focus of his life.

Happy Ralph approaches the finish, the crowd rises in anticipation, and he sails across the line for another spectacular summer win. The thrilled crowd sighs. The mechanical rabbit folds in on itself and disappears. Happy Ralph scampers alongside his trainer in the cool-down jog and receives the coveted victor's vanilla wafers.

Within an hour, Happy Ralph is back in his kennel cage, locked in, alone in the silent darkness.

Since ancient times, people have marveled at the beauty and wonder of the greyhound in full flight. Greyhound images decorated the tombs of the ancient Egyptian pharaohs, and greyhounds are the only dog breed mentioned in the Bible.

In medieval Europe, greyhounds like Happy Ralph were reserved only for the well-born. British gentry used greyhounds for hunting and coursing, a sport in which a pair of greyhounds chase down a rabbit in an enclosed field and are judged on their speed, agility, and grace in running down their prey.

In North America, too, greyhounds were first associated with the upper classes. By the early 1800s, they were used more commonly to keep the newly cleared fields of the American Midwest free of crop-hungry gophers and rabbits. Being sight hounds, they don't sniff out their prey, as most dogs do, but rely on their keen eyesight to detect movement. Reaching speeds of forty-two miles per hour, roughly the same as thoroughbred racehorses, and using their quick intelligence and remarkable agility, they simply outran, out-maneuvered, and outthought their prey. As a symbol of power and grace for the wealthy, and as a useful range dog for farmers, greyhounds found a secure home in nineteenth-century North America. Unfortunately, the industrial age of the twentieth century has not been as kind to them.

People have always raced dogs in county fairs and in special coursing events, but commercial dog racing didn't start until the early 1900s, with the invention of the mechanical rabbit. Greyhound racing had been tried in England with a mechanical lure on a straight track, which didn't work as a spectator sport. The mechanical rabbit was then adapted to an oval track, creating a venue similar to horse racing. Greyhound racing caught on with the public and, more significantly, with gamblers.

For track owners, dogs have a number of advantages over horses. First, dogs can be housed in tiny 30-by-36-by-42-inch cages, stacked one on top of the other. Feed costs are kept low by buying high-protein slaughterhouse refuse. Most important, the dogs are easy to mass produce—a single greyhound female is capable of producing six to eight puppies every year for ten years or more. The industry's puppy mills can cheaply mass produce large volumes of racing product. Greyhounds, companions to pharaohs and kings, have become cogs in the international dog racing machine.

But, like the nuclear power industry, the greyhound racing industry has always had a problem disposing of its waste. This is a young dog's sport. The productive racing age for greyhounds is between eighteen months and five years. The industry's solution has been to euthanize tens of thousands of racing dogs each year, either chemically, electrically, or simply by shooting them as soon as they move from the asset to liability side of the ledger.

Run for Your Life

Happy Ralph watches alertly as the trainer passes his cage without filling his food bowl. This is the first sign that sometime during the morning he will be heading across the parking area to the track. Fidgety, he gets up, stretches, stands, and stares at the door, sits, lies down, gets up, stretches, and looks back at the door. For Happy Ralph, the thrill of race day lies not only in the chance to run, it is the only time he gets out of his cramped quarters for more than a few minutes at a time. Except for the twice-weekly races, he spends all his life, twenty-two hours a day, locked up in a cage less than three feet square.

Happy Ralph's tail beats an excited greeting when the trainer approaches with his racing muzzle and numbered blanket.

From the age of three months, when he lost his generic puppy look and began to develop the greyhound's characteristic slender muzzle and long legs, Happy Ralph's life was an almost unvarying routine of daily feedings, brief stints in the exercise pen, and racing. At six months, the routine was modified by the addition of a plastic jug pulled on a string. With his strong sight-hound instinct and athletic ability, Happy Ralph learned to excel at chasing and hunting down fast-moving inanimate objects.

At ten months, Happy Ralph had proved his potential. He then began to train in earnest, first following a battery-powered drag lure on the straights, then executing high-speed turns chasing a circling whirligig. By his first birth-day, he was pursuing mechanical rabbits around simulated tracks. When he mastered the quick starting break, and could focus all his energy and atten-tion on the lure, Happy Ralph was offered for sale on the racing circuit's open market. He was bought by a speculator who paid for Happy Ralph's upkeep and handling and split his earnings with the racing kennel. His new owner never actually met him.

Happy Ralph mingles with the other dogs in the holding pen under the stands. Like him, most are veterans of hundreds of competitions, but the excitement of the race is still in the air. The dogs mill about like athletes before a big game, offering each other friendly, distracted greetings, focusing on the upcoming event.

Happy Ralph bounds to the starting gate, as ready and eager to race as he was three years earlier, when his wins dominated the track. The gun blasts. He explodes from the gate, but is no longer the first dog out. He runs like the wind, but now there are faster winds around him. By the time he hits his stride, four other dogs are between him and the lure. Once again, he is in fifth place.

It is not an easy place to be. Speeding dogs bump and bruise him as they jostle for position. Happy Ralph has learned to hug the rail for safety, but still the claws of the dog hot on his heels gouge the back of his legs.

Happy Ralph slips back to sixth place as the eight greyhounds approach the final turn. In the last hundred yards, he finds the opening on the rail he has been looking for. He pours it on, ears flat against his head, heart pound-ing, every muscle straining. He should be streaking past the dogs in front, but he isn't. He slips back to the seventh spot. Uncoiling every ounce of power in his aging muscles for a final burst, he finishes the race dead last.

Gamblers who put money on Happy Ralph to win, place, or show crum-ple and throw away their betting slips before the race is over. After a four-year racing career that brought in more than $100,000 in prize money, Happy Ralph is on his way out. In the unforgiving ethos of the racetrack, only two alternatives remain for a five-year-old greyhound who doesn't pay: death or, for a small minority, adoption.

The next morning, Happy Ralph watches the kennel trainer approach his cage with a leash and his muzzle, but no racing blanket. He is led from his kennel to the parking lot and loaded into a van with six other older or injured greyhounds.

The van heads out of the parking lot.

The dog who lived to race looks at his fellow greyhounds with fearful eyes, not knowing where he is going or why.

Strangers wash him, removing ticks and fleas. House, furniture, rugs, even basics like windows are new and unfamiliar. After the dim shed he lived in, this halfway house is a dizzying world of lights, action, and unexpected freedom of movement.

Happy Ralph is carefully tended and rechristened, simply, Ralph. Yet despite the gentle ministrations of his guardians from the greyhound rescue organization, he has difficulty adjusting. Some of the dogs adapt quickly, greeting humans affectionately and exploring the stairs, pantry, and making wonderful discoveries, like couches. But Ralph hangs back, still surrounded by an imaginary 30-by-36-by-42-inch cage. Finding no place for himself in a world without bars, he lies on a blanket on the floor, hoping to stay out of harm's way.

For one long week, he watches and waits.

Until, one sunny morning, Ralph makes his own great discovery.

He discovers Pat.

·   ·   ·

Pat Cloutier visits Ralph's transition house after reading a greyhound rescue pamphlet at a dog show. Rescue organizations say that thirty thousand North American greyhounds are being killed by kennel owners each year, although the industry association puts the figure at around seven thousand. Pat learns that rescue operations springing up across the continent take as many dogs as they can place in homes and foster homes and save fifteen thousand greyhounds a year. With her children grown, Pat comes to see what she can nurture next.

Half a dozen thin greyhounds crowd around her, nudging her gently with their slender muzzles to make physical contact, their tails beating a happy rhythm on the walls and door. One dog, coal black and quiet, with a serious look, holds back. Only after the other dogs move off does he approach timidly. Pat doesn't know why Ralph is drawn to her. Perhaps it is her tone of voice, or that he is finally ready to explore his new world.

Ralph nuzzles her tentatively in a friendly but cautious greeting.

Pat Cloutier has the compelling feeling that this dark greyhound has chosen her. She came with her husband, Roger, to learn more about rescuing greyhounds. She leaves with Ralph sitting quietly on the backseat, heading home.

The first few days, Ralph moves through the house with delicate, deerlike steps. Greyhounds are large dogs, but after spending all his life in a small cage, Ralph has learned to take up minimum space. His favorite place is on the couch beside Roger, where he curls up tightly, folding his lanky limbs and long torso into a compact ball.

Outdoors, he treats other dogs and children with a gentleness that belies his great size. When other dogs are aggressive, he shrugs them off without fear, showing a dignified sense of forbearance.

Three days after his arrival, Ralph greets Pat's husband, running to him as he returns from work. Then something kicks in and Ralph keeps on running, around the lilac bush, the in-ground pool, the clump of maples, taking the turn at full speed, and heading back around the lilac bush for a second lap. Pat and Roger watch in amazement as the swift, sleek creature streaks by them, the only lure being the release of a flat-out, ears-back, heart-pounding, exuberant run.

Five years after he discovered Pat, Ralph's black muzzle is slowly turning white. He lies in the shade of the lilac bush in Pat's backyard with his female companion, Black Taffy, another rescued greyhound, stretched out by his side. Three newly arrived greyhounds, Molly Mudhen, PS McCarlo, and Hit the Buzzer, sprawl in the shade of the house.

Now, at the age of ten, Ralph has a touch of arthritis that slows him down, but it doesn't prevent his regular runs on the track he has beaten around the edge of the lawn. Answering a call that goes back in time, long

before the invention of a fake rabbit, Ralph awakens from a snooze on the grass, stretches his long limbs, and begins to run. The other greyhounds react as if a gun went off, leaping to their feet to follow the old champion, who is happily flying around a suburban backyard on a greyhound-owned and -operated racetrack—Happy Ralph, white-whiskered and triumphant, once again in the lead.

. . . .

ONTARIO, CANADA

MEL

Mel looks up with devoted calm at Laurie Campbell and sneaks a quick glance at the toy mouse in her pocket. His interest peaks as Laurie wiggles its colorful tail and makes it squeak. Eyes bright with excitement, mouth open and panting, Mel is excited and ready for action.

Laurie gives Mel a last-minute primp with the ever-ready steel comb, untucked from her armband. Momentarily, he forgets about the toy and kowtows to Laurie, leisurely stretching his front legs.

"I love you, too," Laurie murmurs. "Too bad I know it's really the rodent you're after and not me."

The ringmaster announces their number and the duo prepares for their entrance in the best in show competition, the climactic moment of the weekend dog show.

Black coat gleaming in the hot July sun, Mel struts into the ring looking positively electric. His manicured, pedicured, shampooed, clipped, snipped, and hair-sprayed body prances with effortless grace. With his lionesque mane held proudly aloft, and his shaved and pom-pomed muscular hindquarters shining in the sun, Mel is the picture-perfect image of a classic standard poodle.

The standard is the biggest and oldest of the three types of poodle—toy, miniature, and standard. At the shoulder, they measure between twenty-two and twenty-six inches—Mel's height. Laurie feels they get a bad rap "because of the funny haircut, the hair spray, and because they're so pampered." In fact, the word "poodle" derives from the German word *puddeln,* meaning "to splash in water." Originally a water dog and retriever of water game, the poodle is closely related to the Portuguese water dog and the Irish water spaniel.

Mel's officially registered show name is American Canadian Champion Vetset Forever Young. Vetset is the name of the renowned poodle-breeding kennel run by Mel's owner, veterinarian Elly Holowaychuk. It's also home to Mel's dam, Ascot's Nice n' Easy, who was bred to Kaylen's Cadillac Style, a multiple best in show winner in the United States, to produce Mel.

Under the care of professional handler Laurie Campbell, Mel is jockeying to reach the pinnacle of purebred beauty and win the coveted conformation title Top Dog in Canada. At the tender age of three, he's entering the prime of his show-dog career. Accumulating points and best in show ribbons is the name of the game. Ten or more best in show wins means a run at being Top Dog. With the upcoming high-profile Limestone City Obedience & Kennel Club Show, Laurie and Mel are hoping to add to the thirteen they already have.

This is Mel's year and he's hot.

In Working Trim

The morning they leave for the show, Mel hops obediently into the raised bathtub in Laurie's roomy tunnel-shaped kennel. The grooming area is lined with a mass of cleaning and conditioning potions and trimming instruments. Laurie's favorite country-western music and intermittent barking from the dozen other occupants fill the air. A sack of show ribbons overflows the counter onto the floor.

Gone is Mel's wild-dog demeanor of the night before when he romped through Laurie's hillside acreage in southern Ontario. He had sported blue plastic wrappers on his ten-inch ears to keep his fur clean, dry, and out of his mouth, and his massive head of hair was tied in three samurai-like topknots. He gamboled alongside Laurie until a rustle in the underbrush drew him away. When he finally emerged, jumping up on her and licking, Laurie was aghast to see sticky burrs obscuring his thick coat. She quickly ushered him to the grooming area for an emergency desnagging session, still convinced the play-mess trade-off was thoroughly worthwhile. "They're dogs first, part of the family, and then they're precious little statues in the ring. And many a judge has commented on Mel's beautiful muscle tone as well as the condition of his hair."

Mel's eyes squint shut as Laurie douses his thick coat and applies shampoo. She works up a good lather and quietly orders him to present his other side. Mel obeys, cocking his head helpfully to let Laurie rinse his ear. "From start to finish, just the preshow bath and groom, you're looking at between five and six hours devoted to one darling little dog."

After the final rinse, Mel shakes thoroughly on command and Laurie stands away from the flying droplets. His body balloons into a thick mass of tight miniature ringlets. With only his snout visible, Laurie is reminded how the poodle clip came into being for these water retrievers. "It's actually a working trim. The dogs were getting waterlogged. They couldn't swim. So they started cutting off what wasn't necessary."

Wrapped in a big terry cloth towel, Mel cocoons in Laurie's arms as she walks to the grooming table to begin the drying procedures. He stands patiently as she blasts off the excess water with an air hose. Then he luxuriates, lying down and dozing off as Laurie, using a freestanding industrial-strength hair dryer, patiently combs and dries every single recalcitrant hair into straightened submission.

Mel's coat is now fluffed into a floating black cloud, his head fur back in its usual topknots and blue ear wrappers. Awake now and poised on the grooming table, Mel turns and shifts pliantly, allowing Laurie liberal access with the clipper to even his most intimate private parts. As she shaves with impeccable artistry, she reveals the origins and evolution of the poodle clip. "Fur bracelets to cover the pasterns and the hocks, rosettes on the hips to cover the hip joints and the kidneys. The tail is used as a rudder, so a pompom keeps it warm. And then the big coat covers the vital organs. But we take everything to extremes, so this is what we end up with."

Mel's feet are last to be shaved, and his thick dark nails are clipped short to obtain the required standard poodle contour. Laurie splays his toes as she works. The deep webbing linking each digit is ideal for water dogs like standard poodles, whose swimming abilities extend to the very tips of their toes.

A final comb and dry ends Mel's preliminary grooming session. Laurie leads him out of dirt and harm's way to his outdoor run. Her "star" now primped, she quickly grooms the seven other dogs accompanying them to the show.

Laurie swings open the side door of her metallic gray stretch van. Inside, neatly packed, are dog crates, plastic feed bins, hair dryers, grooming kits, grooming tables, tarps, collapsible exercise pens, and even a supply of water to avoid unpredictable tummy upsets from strange drinking water. Now that they're into the "campaigning" stage of Mel's career, chalking up show points, Mel and Laurie will spend more than two hundred days on the road together, traveling from coast to coast. His grooming calm forgotten, Mel prances, tongue and tail wagging eagerly as Laurie escorts him to the van.

The van pulls into Lake Ontario Park, Kingston, at nightfall. The parking lot is crammed with vehicles and trailers, many of them sleek, mammoth models with humming generators. Mel and Laurie greet the other regulars on the dog-show circuit, a subculture Laurie knows well. Her mother was a professional dog handler and Laurie grew up on the road, in scenes like this. Dogs are everywhere—in carpeted, shaded pens, being walked and groomed, barking, peeking out from stacks of cages inside trucks and vans— a total of eight hundred dogs by Saturday, the busiest day.

Mel watches the commotion quietly from the comfort of his cage while Laurie sets up their open-sided grooming tent, tables, equipment and feed, preparing for the coming three-day marathon.

They both sleep soundly in a nearby motel, with Mel comfortably settled at the foot of Laurie's bed.

· · ·

In the morning, Mel paces himself like an old pro. His first event isn't until 2:30 P.M. But after that, the competition will be intense.

Being a standard poodle, Mel belongs to the non-sporting category, the most varied group of dogs, including breeds as diverse as the sturdy French bulldog and the snub-nosed, silky-haired Lhasa apso. The other six categories are sporting, hound, working, terrier, toy, and herding.

If Mel wins the standard poodle event for best of breed, he'll go on to enter the competition for best of group. If he wins that, he competes for best in show, and that title is Mel and Laurie's cherished weekend objective.

Mel rises from a leisurely nap in his cage and unwinds calmly in his ex, or exercise pen, barely noticing the flow of dogs and handlers to and from the main competition tent at the heart of the site. With the thermometer and humidity climbing steadily, the line at the lemonade stand doubles.

"Wanna play?" Laurie teases Mel. She's had a full morning, showing a sweet golden retriever puppy for its first time, a soft-coated wheaten terrier, and an unexpected last-minute showing of a Cavalier King Charles spaniel. The rest of her day is devoted to the real work, getting Mel ready for competition.

Mel balances his forelegs on the grooming table. "Stay," Laurie commands as she heaves the rest of him up. "Good boy."

Fully attentive, Mel waits on the table, mouth open, panting lightly. Laurie gathers her beauty tools—a flat rectangular grooming brush and a bottle of light conditioner. It's a familiar ritual to Mel. Laurie moves to her grooming stool.

Mel's shimmering coat gets a final thorough brushing and spraying to keep every hair in place. Laurie finesses Mel's crowning glory, his topknot, as activity in her shared tent intensifies. Handlers come and go, borrowing items, leaving dogs in her care, using up a corner of her precious space to set up their own grooming tables or ex pens. Mel is an island of concentrated calm in a sea of endless movement. "He's so good, he seems to sense when I'm starting to get a little stressed and he behaves better."

Mel closes his eyes as Laurie sprays his topknot into a perfect fountain of straight black hair. Then he stands patiently for the final scissoring, which renders him the absolute model of poodle clip roundness and smoothness.

Hair spray in hand, steel comb tucked into her numbered armband, Laurie heads off to the show ring. On his custom-made kangaroo-hide leash, Mel prances proudly alongside her like a tightly wound thoroughbred. "Mel's a real showman. He's really good until we start to approach ringside, then he gets excited because he wants to get in there."

Mel fidgets under the shady main tent as the miniature poodles finish in the ring. Laurie teases him with his favorite toy mouse to keep him keyed up, psyching him into a show-dog frame of mind. The unbearable humidity adds to the tension. Huge banks of threatening clouds blanket the sky.

Finally, it's show time.

Mel and Laurie line up with the other competitors—ten standard poodles presented in groups of three and four. Laurie focuses Mel's attention totally on her and the toy mouse while they wait their turn. By the time the ringmaster calls their number, they're perfectly in sync.

It's a "good hair day" for Mel and he looks exceptional. Most of the other competitors sport the more conservative English saddle clip, which hides chunks of their physique under thick, neatly trimmed coats. Mel's continental clip, with its extensive shaved areas, is obviously more high-maintenance, but perfect for the exquisite build and muscle tone he has to flaunt.

Mel and Laurie lope effortlessly around the ring with three fellow competitors. Hands on hips, the judge focuses intently on each dog circling around each one, comparing them individually to the established breed standard. "They go over the body structure, the conditioning—coat and muscle tone," Laurie explains. "Presentation is obviously part of it. Temperament is a very big part. It's kind of a Miss America for dogs, except they don't have to sing, dance, or twirl batons."

The judge's hands examine Mel's body, feeling for structural flaws and muscle tone. Laurie watches closely. It's her policy to handle only "sound" or healthy dogs, like Mel. Attempts to achieve the ideal show dog by linebreeding, or inbreeding, can lead to structural weaknesses, serious hereditary diseases, and a shortened life span. Lack of genetic diversity has contaminated certain standard poodle lineages with inherited epilepsy and bloat, a potentially fatal gastrointestinal condition. Ellie Holowaychuk uses judicious breeding practices,

never mating dogs within the same lineage to each other. Mel is sound, not plagued by the cost of his beauty.

The judge asks Mel and Laurie to make a solo pass out into the ring. Then he moves on to the next dog.

Mel and Laurie whiz through the last group run and head back to the shade of the tent.

The judge points wordlessly at them.

They've got it. First place—best of breed!

As if he knows there's more to come, Mel remains surprisingly calm— until he spots a familiar face in the crowd. It's the owner of the first female standard poodle Mel was bred with. Seeing her brings back such sweet, intoxicating memories that Mel's show demeanor completely evaporates. In a flash, he's all over the unsuspecting woman, a black enveloping amorous cloud, almost knocking her off her lawn chair.

"All right, Mel, all right!" Laurie chides him, laughing. "Yes, you're a good boy!"

Ears returned to their protective blue wrappers, Mel waits at ringside. His eyes don't leave Laurie for a second as she shows a Tibetan spaniel for another client. When she gives the spaniel a departing kiss on the snout, he seems to shoot her a dirty look, and timely thunder rumbles from the darkening skies.

Then it's back to the ring for best in group. Mel and Laurie are up against a miniature poodle, a shar-pei, a chow chow, a Lhasa apso, a bulldog, a dalmatian, a schipperke, a Boston terrier, a löwchen, and a shiba inu.

The skies open, it starts to pour, and the competitors move under the awning. The trainers pose their dogs, showing off their best features. Some use food; others, like Laurie, a favorite toy—anything to keep the dogs still and focused. The tension builds. Eyeing a red first-place ribbon on the table beside them, Laurie whispers, "See this one, Mel? I want one of those."

The competition progresses. One by one, the judge eliminates the minia-ture poodle, the dalmatian, the Boston terrier, the Lhasa apso, and the shiba inu.

Mel shakes himself off as he and Laurie return to the awning after their last group run. He's keyed up and so is Laurie.

The judge points in rapid-fire succession first to Mel, then to the three other dogs: one, two, three, and four.

Mel and Laurie have won again! Mel jumps up exuberantly on Laurie as if to say: "We did it!"

On a grooming table under the big tent, Mel is treated to a last-minute primp. Spirits run high as the various camps position themselves around the ring for the pinnacle of the first day, the best in show competition. It's a com-petition of winners. Mel has won the non-sporting group for the day and his six fellow competitors have all won in their respective categories.

The normally subdued audience claps and hoots as the champion show dogs make their entrances: the Pomeranian, Mel, the Bouvier des Flandres, and the other winners.

Mel is pumped up, maybe too much. He can't contain himself any longer. He leaps up on Laurie right in front of the judge.

"Stop that!" Laurie scolds. But it's too late.

The Pomeranian wins the day.

Laurie changes from her show-ring dress suit into shorts and a T-shirt, her favorite "hurtin' music" playing on the radio. Mel, one paw elegantly draped over the corner of the grooming table, rests quietly as she combs out his spray-laden locks.

They haven't done too badly, really, for the first day. The dog-show world is unpredictable and tomorrow brings another set of competitions with a different judge. As she painstakingly combs Mel's hair for the zillionth time, Laurie smiles, remembering a much younger Mel.

"As soon as he walked out of the crate, I knew he was going to be a star. And when I showed him for the first time, he was absolutely the wildest dog I'd ever shown. Totally undisciplined, almost dragged me around the ring. He was so ecstatic to be there."

She kisses him on his well-coiffed snout.

The next day, Mel beats the Pomeranian and adds a fourteenth best in show rosette to his blossoming collection.

. . . .

BRITISH COLUMBIA, CANADA

KAVIK

The big timber wolf moves through the shadows at the edge of the clearing, stopping for a moment to peer through the branches. His yellow-flecked eyes shine in the moonlight. He catches a faint scent in the air, stiffens, then crouches to wait. There is a rustle in the branches above. The wolf looks up. A tribesman lets the arrow fly and the wolf drops in its tracks.

A triumphant shout breaks the silence. The director of *The Sentinel,* a television series produced by Paramount, emerges from behind the bushes pleased to have filmed this shot in one take.

Steve Woodley, standing just off camera, is also pleased.

"Good boy," he calls. "Good boy, Kavik."

At the sound of his trainer's voice, the mortally wounded wolf suddenly transforms into a big playful dog. He leaps up and bounds to Steve for praise and a slice of garlic chicken, his favorite treat. Steve rubs Kavik's neck and checks to make sure he didn't injure himself in the scene.

In a flurry of activity on the set, technicians move the camera dolly, electricians adjust the lighting, and a propwoman approaches Steve and Kavik holding a belt-and-arrow contraption at arm's length. She gingerly offers it to Steve, giving the big canine a wide berth. Kavik is a wolf dog, half timber wolf, half Alaskan malamute, but his yellow eyes and powerful movements suggest more wolf than dog.

Steve fits the elastic with the half arrow around Kavik's chest for the dying wolf shot and ruffles his ears. Kavik thumps his tail happily and then, on cue, obediently drops dead.

Wolf dogs are a rare breed today, but they have existed for tens of thousands of years, ever since dog and wolf first parted ways.

In some parts of the world, such as Italy, wolves have bred with stray dogs for centuries and wild packs of wolf dogs roam rural areas, threatening livestock. The wholesale slaughter of wolves in North America has curtailed their interactions with dogs in populated areas, but thousands of wolf dogs are bred in captivity each year as pets. In some states, wolf-dog hybrids are classed as domestic animals. In other states, such as Washington, where Kavik was bred, wolf dogs are listed along with lions and tigers as exotic animals and regulations require almost zoo-like conditions for keeping them.

Wolf dog advocates insist that wolf dogs are no more dangerous than any other big, powerful breed. Detractors point out that in the last two decades, more than a dozen people in the United States have been killed in wolf dog attacks. Steve Woodley, Kavik's highly experienced trainer, prefers to err on the side of caution. "Kavik is a great animal," he says, "but this breed is not for everyone. You have to know what you are doing. There are instincts in wolf dogs that you don't want to awaken."

A Dog in Wolf's Clothing

The sun rises over the farmland and suburbs of British Columbia's lower mainland, and Kavik moves to the front of his pen, listening for sounds from the house. He hears the first stirrings of Steve's indoor dogs and his tail begins to wag. Finally, Steve approaches his backyard pen, and the large wolf dog wriggles and gyrates like a frisky puppy. The minute Steve opens the gate, Kavik rushes forward with his characteristic wolfish grin and presses his flank into Steve's leg, almost toppling him over with his bulk.

After their ritual morning greeting, Steve releases Kavik into the four-acre fenced-in field behind the house. Using his fine nose to read the night's animal traffic, Kavik trots from gopher hole to rabbit warren, stopping to sniff the markings left by the other dogs and diligently adding his own. A slight movement in the grass attracts his keen eye. He freezes, lowers to a

crouch, and straightens—it's only a field mouse. Halfway across the field, Kavik suddenly explodes, fast and straight as a bullet. A rabbit barely makes it to the safety of its den. The wolf dog crisscrosses the field, heading to the end of the enclosure where he sometimes catches the intoxicating scent of deer. He trots along the fence with his nose in the air, reading the wind.

Steve considers these morning runs Kavik's private wolf time, an opportunity for him to stretch his strong limbs and patrol his territory. But when he calls Kavik in to work, it's Kavik the dog he wants to see.

At the sound of Steve's voice, the big canine stops, tilts his head, then lopes in long graceful strides toward the house.

Five-year-old Kavik has been living with Steve Woodley almost all his adult life. Kavik's original owner, dismayed when his small cuddly puppy metamorphosed into a giant 140-pound animal, desperately advertised for someone to take him away. Steve and his boss, Mark Dumas, owner of Creative Animal Talent, answered the ad. They specialized in training grizzly bears, polar bears, and dogs for TV and film work. A canine with a strong wolfish appearance was a natural asset to their furry stable. When he first saw him, Steve blanched at Kavik's awesome size. He had been training German shepherds and huskies, but Kavik, with his powerful shoulders and massive chest, was bigger again by half. His wide forehead, long pointy snout, and narrow amber-flecked eyes were also daunting. Steve's first reaction was to back away. But then Kavik wagged his tail and his face took on the inoffensive, self-deprecating look of a dog that wants you to like him. "I knew at second glance," Steve says, "that Kavik was an animal I could work with."

This morning, Steve warms up Kavik for his new role, starring in the TV adaptation of Jack London's classic *The Call of the Wild*. Kavik will be playing Buck, a former house pet who was stolen, abused, and forced into service as a sled dog.

On command, Kavik sits. Steve moves backward, hand extended, rolling his fingers in the slow pace signal. Kavik creeps forward as if he's stalking prey. Steve holds his hand flat up, like a traffic cop. Kavik freezes on an imaginary mark. Steve holds his palm face up and pulls his fingers inward in the move-up-a-bit sign. Kavik moves up two paces and stops. Then, with a wave of his trainer's arm, Kavik is launched. He leaps at Steve and lands full force, paws planted on his chest. Steve praises Kavik as he gently lowers him back to the ground. The big wolf dog stays put until Steve gives him the drop-dead signal. Kavik flops over dramatically. This is his all-time favorite trick, one he never tires of performing.

Kavik was bewildered when he first came to Steve, but he picked up basic dog obedience in record time. Steve was encouraged to find that the wolf dog had all the essential ingredients of a good working dog: a desire to please, a boundless hunger for treats, and a quick intelligence. Kavik soon moved on to the more complicated hand commands used in his work. Like most tame wolves, he was better at responding to these nonverbal signals than most dogs.

Even more crucial than the pace of Kavik's training was his socialization. Animal actors are in constant contact with crowds, and Steve had to be sure his new acquisition was trustworthy. Although Kavik instantly took to Steve's wife, recognizing her as an important part of the household, getting him used to new people took careful planning. Steve handed out garlic chicken treats to all his friends and anyone else willing to approach the big wolf dog until Kavik learned to expect great things from strangers.

Once Kavik was fully at ease, Steve began to test his reactions to stressful situations. He would shove him gently, surprise him with sudden movements, and shout loud commands to re-create the chaos of the set. Each time he reassured and rewarded his pupil and Kavik came to accept these bizarre human habits.

There remained one final test for Kavik. How would he react to Steve's two children? Some dogs are threatened by a child's unpredictable movements or consider themselves superior in the family hierarchy to the tiny humans. Steve and his wife observed Kavik intently for the slightest sign of aggression or unease. But to both parents' surprise, Kavik showed immediate and unreserved affection for the small children. Soon, the wolf dog was happily prowling around the room with Steve's seven-year-old son riding on his back.

With Kavik's human socialization well established, Steve felt it was time to introduce him to his other dogs—in particular to Primo, the dominant male dog in the household, who would play his TV rival, Spitz, in *The Call of the Wild*. The German shepherd was instantly suspicious of the new canine invading his territory. Primo circled the newcomer while Steve watched for Kavik's reaction. The big wolf dog showed complete unconcern. Primo moved in to sniff him more closely. Kavik gave him a friendly wag and looked away. At this sign of submission, Steve realized with relief that Primo, half the size of Kavik, would not have to fight to preserve his top dog position in the house.

Steve releases Primo into the backyard so he and Kavik can prepare for their climactic scene, scheduled to shoot that afternoon. In this scene, Buck, repeatedly tormented by Spitz, the lead sled dog he has displaced, finally fights back.

Kavik bounds forward delightedly to greet his chum. The dogs run, whirl, and collide as they race around the yard, taking turns chasing each other. After a few minutes, the game gets a bit rough. Kavik is following hard on Primo's heels when the German shepherd turns sharply and the wolf dog crashes into him. Primo spins around, bares his teeth, and growls a warning. Steve sees a split-second flash of fang from Kavik. This is precisely what he has to re-create for the fight scene, but his heart skips a beat. Steve is unsure what will follow Kavik's first snarl. Will the well-socialized dog's respect for authority kick in? Or will something deep-rooted and dangerous erupt from behind those yellow eyes? If Kavik becomes truly angry, he could rip Primo apart in minutes.

Kavik quickly regains his composure, pins his ears back apologetically, and looks away, avoiding confrontation.

The playful chase resumes.

In the Bordertown Studio, on the *Call of the Wild* set, Kavik readies for his cue. On command, the big wolf dog slowly circles the crouching German shepherd whose eyes are filled with fear and fury. The German shepherd curls his lip and strikes, desperately trying to drive off his opponent. The wolf dog deftly steps aside, lowers his head menacingly, and moves in for the kill. Just as he seems poised to leap at the German shepherd's throat, the director yells "Cut," and announces a long-awaited break.

"Good boy, Kavik. Good boy, Primo," calls Steve, standing just off-camera.

The two canines bound forward to receive their garlic chicken treats, and several cast members detour around Kavik to pat Primo.

Primo socializes with the crew while Kavik receives an affectionate rubdown from Steve. "You're just a big goof, Kavik," Steve says, and the giant wolf dog, as if to prove the point, bounces up and down on his forelegs in the universal canine invitation to play.

Kavik and Primo stretch out in the shade as Steve flips through his notes for the major fight sequence. He is pleased with his dogs' earlier performance. Both had remained alert and focused on his dancing puppeteer-like hands, connected to him as if by invisible strings.

The next scene calls for the two adversaries to fight to the death. As would be the outcome of a real-life fight between the 140-pound Kavik and the ninety-pound Primo, Buck is scripted to make quick work of Spitz.

Steve mentally rehearses the complicated fight sequence. Since Primo is actually the dominant canine, the fight-to-the-death has to be choreographed and handled with great care. It requires absolute confidence in Kavik's and Primo's ability to act professionally and control themselves. They must give the impression of tearing each other apart without ever crossing the line into reality.

Steve looks up from his notes and notices the renewed activity around the set.

"Let's go, guys," he calls, and Kavik and Primo rise immediately to their feet and trot dutifully into the circle of cameras, lights, and cables.

Steve shows them to their marks and Kavik and Primo fix their eyes on Steve's magic hands. The cast and crew members crowd around to watch the dramatic dog fight scene.

"Silence on the set," calls the assistant director.

Steve lowers his left hand. Kavik crouches. The trainer rolls his fingers. Kavik creeps toward Primo, who stands his ground, ears back and lips curled. With the added soundtrack of a deep menacing growl, the German shepherd's expression will appear almost demonic.

Steve holds up his hand to Kavik, who freezes on his new mark. Kavik's face shows his intense concentration. Edited into a fast-paced fight scene, his look will seem like cold fury.

Kavik watches Steve's hand, held palm upward, making a grabbing motion. He moves up two paces and stops. The two canines are now less than three feet apart. The tension on the set is tangible. With Primo's white teeth bared and spittles of saliva pooling at the corners of his mouth, it seems to the cast and crew that they are about to witness a vicious fight. Steve gives Primo the leap sign. The German shepherd gathers himself and hurtles through the air, landing squarely on Kavik's back. For a second, Kavik hesitates, motionless. Steve's hands continue moving and Kavik twirls around to free himself.

The trainer notices the shadow of stress in Kavik's eyes. Kavik is a good-natured animal, but tolerating a frothing, ninety-pound, dominant dog on his back is a lot to ask.

Steve's left hand carves an arc through the air. Kavik shakes off Primo and wheels around to face him again. Steve gives Kavik the snarl sign and the big wolf dog shows his frightening fangs. Two extras, watching from the sidelines, step back.

Now it's time for the kill. Steve rolls his hand and Kavik moves in. The two canines meet chest-to-chest, ears back and teeth flashing. They rise on their hind legs, biting, aiming for the coveted throat hold. Primo feints right

and drops his shoulder, trying to sink his teeth into Kavik's foreleg. They lose their balance and roll in the grassy field. Kavik finishes on top, his jaws just inches from Primo's neck. He freezes there.

This final part of the sequence is the most stressful for the animals because it calls for an inversion of their established dominance. Primo, the alpha male, is on his back, with his normally submissive housemate at his neck. Both animals hold their positions as the cameras roll.

"It's a keeper," exults the director.

"Good boy, Primo. Good boy, Kavik." Steve praises them with relief. Instantly, the tension evaporates. Kavik and Primo, friends again, romp over to Steve for well-deserved treats. Perhaps sensing that these few film minutes represent weeks of work, the cast and crew break into spontaneous applause.

The two canine actors relax a moment before starting the grueling work of breaking down the scene into individual close-ups and reaction shots to ensure that the editor has enough footage to make the sequence flow. By the end of the afternoon, Kavik is deliberately misinterpreting the signals, his way of evading a command, and Steve knows that his wolf dog star is tired and bored. It's time to call it a day.

That evening, back home, Kavik and Primo luxuriate in rubdowns and a relaxing spray shower, Steve's version of a canine spa. Primo, his character now deceased and his role over, stretches out comfortably on Steve's plush living-room carpet.

As he does every night before going to bed, Steve goes out back for one last visit with Kavik. The gentle giant's tail drums excitedly on the wire mesh of his pen as Steve approaches. His trainer strokes his head and speaks to him softly. "You're really just a big goof," Steve says. The wolf dog gazes up at him in complicity. "And now you're a huge television star." Kavik responds to the affectionate tone with another wolfish grin.

Sometime around midnight, while the Vancouver bedroom community sleeps, a police siren wails faintly at the other end of town. Suddenly, the suburb resounds with the mournful, unmistakable howling of the wolf in Steve Woodley's backyard. The haunting sound continues long after the siren fades, but with prolonged pauses between the howls, as Kavik listens for a reply. For Steve, this is part of the wonder of Kavik, the big canine who lives and works with domestic dogs, but who still sings, from deep inside, the wolf's wild, long-forgotten song.

PART FOUR

SLED DOGS

. . . .

ELMER

Elmer's team begins the slow turn onto the 22 Mile Bend of the Yukon River, leading the competition by a few hours. Elmer managed to buy them this slim margin over the past week of tough sledding. His muscular, square-set body led the powerful Alaskan huskies across the rough terrain of Finger Lake, up Rainy Pass, down the treacherous Dalzell Gorge, and over the hidden stumps of the Burn. Sixteen dogs in harness, each pulling hard, and Elmer kept the towline taut and the team on track, picking out a clean course and avoiding open water and rocks. He had become Doug Swingley's lead sled dog in the 1995 Iditarod. That year, they won the grueling race in nine days, two hours, forty-two minutes, and nineteen seconds, a record that stands to this day. Now in his sixth Iditarod, eight-year-old Elmer is dean of the sled dogs. If the Iditarod is Alaska's Super Bowl, Elmer is the Joe Montana of sled dogs, the Michael Jordan of the canine world.

Now the team is pulling straight north up Alaska's largest river, battling extreme wind and cold for the second blustery day in a row. For this lap, Elmer runs behind the leaders, in the swing position. In front are his daughter and granddaughter, Stormy and Cola. Elmer pulls hard, effortlessly. He's unhappy about being "rested," and he doesn't like having another dog's tail two feet in front of his face. He wants to lead, but that's no reason to sulk. They all have a job to do—pull the sled, follow the trail, win the race. Their long strides cover more than ten miles an hour, a good pace. Ahead, the white, frozen river stretches for miles.

Then, as the sled heads into the arc of the Yukon River between Eagle Island and Kaltag, they hit the full-force gales of the infamous 22 Mile Bend wind. Freezing winter winds shriek inland through Kotzebue Sound, funneled by the Kaiyuh and Kaltag Mountains. A ferocious ground blizzard, powered by the wind and fueled by the soft powder on the riverbanks, surrounds the sled.

The snow swirls and the dog team loses all sense of space and orientation.

Blinded, the lead dogs veer into the bank, seeking shelter. Doug realizes that he is about to lose his first-place position, maybe the race.

But one dog keeps on pulling straight ahead.

It's Elmer, and he wants to lead.

Elmer's powerful drive to pull, run, and lead finds its roots in the origins of his breed, the Alaskan husky. The first dogs used as sled dogs were Siberian huskies, developed by the Chukchi, a seminomadic tribe in northeastern Siberia. These dogs could pull a loaded sled for miles in the most severe cold without tiring. The Alaskan husky evolved through crossbreeding these Siberian dogs with the best Canadian huskies, Alaskan malamutes, and native village dogs. Of all working dogs, the Alaskan husky remains the most hybrid of all—an incredible athletic supermutt. Hardiness, endurance, strength, speed, enthusiasm, and problem-solving skills were all bred into the mix. Only beauty and looks were left out of the original Alaskan husky recipe.

But, over time, these sixty- to seventy-pound powerhouses have turned into handsome dogs as well. Elmer's proud, long-limbed posture may derive from genes added from another fine ancient canine athlete—the Egyptian saluki. The origins of this sight hound, its name meaning "the royal one," date back eight thousand years, perhaps making it the first domesticated dog. Salukis were so fast that they outpaced the gazelles in their homeland. To capitalize on this breed's amazing acceleration, they were bred into the sled-dog gene pool at the beginning of the twentieth century.

Alaskan huskies were raised to help humans transport water, food, hunting supplies, freight, and mail. Before modern technology brought the snowmobile and reliable winter air travel to the north, sled dogs provided the doorway to the world beyond for many northern people. From this arose a fascinating interdependency—a people whose way of life depended on a dog, and a dog who could not survive without its human counterpart.

The world-famous Iditarod race commemorates the husky's finest moment. In the particularly harsh winter of 1925, a violent diphtheria epidemic broke out in the coastal city of Nome. The governor of Alaska ordered mushers to report to relay points along the 670 miles between Nenana and Nome to transport life-saving serum to the mortally threatened city. The legendary Serum Run involved twenty dog teams relaying serum along much of what is now the Iditarod trail. Out of this heroic mission arose the legends of Togo and Balto, two lead dogs who pulled their sleds through blanketing whiteouts, one of whom—Balto—is honored with a bronze statue in New York's Central Park.

The Last Great Race

Elmer waits in downtown Anchorage as the sun peeks over the Chugach Mountains. The large, northern city of 250,000, which normally resembles a ghost town at this early hour, is buzzing with activity. In two hours, the Iditarod Sled Dog Race from Anchorage to Nome, traditionally staged on the first Saturday of March, officially begins.

A cacophony of voices, barks, and revving motors fills the streets. Elmer, in his sixth Iditarod, draws his share of attention, but ignores it. Like his trainer, Doug Swingley, he is eager to get out of the city and into the wilderness, where there is, as Doug says, "less distraction." They may face extreme

weather, dog fights, waist-deep snow, exhaustion, and hallucinations crossing the 1,100 miles of Alaska's back country. But it is this inner-city gauntlet before the start of the race that is often the most trying part of the trip.

"Hi, boy!" Doug beams, as Elmer looks at him with undeniable excitement. "Do you want to go for a run?"

Elmer raises his head into the harness in response and then immediately bounds to the front of the line attached to the sled. Every muscle in his tight body quivers with excitement as Doug hooks him to the towline with a small brass snap. The strong husky watches Doug position his fellow team members—all world-class canine athletes in their own right. Following Elmer in the lead, both in the swing position, are Stormy and Cola. Then there's Peppy, Satin and Ceaser, Fungus and Moldy, Hadrian and Ross, Rumble, Gus, Freak, Abby, and Echo and Diesel—frisky huskies ranging in age from three to nine years old.

With minutes left before the race, Elmer stands alertly at the front of his team, undistracted by the thousands of yelling, applauding, whistling spectators, many of whom have brought their family pets.

Ahead lies the tremendous challenge of hauling a 150-pound sled on an arduous marathon across thousands of miles of frozen tundra. In canine terms, the Iditarod is the Ironman triathlon, Mount Everest, and the Tour de France rolled into one.

Elmer leans into his harness as Doug steps onto the runners.

The launch area is a madhouse. Dogs stamp their feet, yelp, bark, and whine in anticipation. They strain against their traces, wanting to run.

"Elmer, stay ahead," Doug mutters. Volunteers hold back Doug's sled. The megaphone blasts the countdown—TEN, NINE, EIGHT...ONE—and the volunteers release their grip.

The dogs' combined excitement transfers into an explosive takeoff. Doug's canine-powered vehicle speeds along the snow-packed trail quietly, deceptively fast. At first, the power and speed are overwhelming, almost reckless.

"Whoa! Take a rest, guys, we have a long way to go," Doug calls out after a few miles. At the same time, he engages the sled brake to provide resistance. Mushing is both science and art, and the musher must be one with his team. Training the dogs to run fast and hard is easy, that's embedded in their genes. Teaching them to pace themselves and stop is more difficult.

Training begins in August and continues until the end of February, when the dogs are loaded into the truck for the long drive from western Montana to Alaska. Doug, their coach, exercises them daily to build up enough muscle early in the season to avoid joint and tissue injuries when speed and steep climbs become critical.

Now, 250 miles outside of Anchorage, all the hard work pays off, as the team runs strong even after the ascent of Rainy Pass. Ahead is the dreaded Dalzell Gorge. Doug and Elmer must guide the team down a steep, winding trail that plunges one thousand feet in only five miles. Elmer's role is key; they're moving so fast that Doug couldn't stop them if he tried. He keeps a watchful eye on his lead dog's behavior—even a slight flicker of Elmer's ears might indicate danger ahead, a log blocking the trail or open water.

Elmer leads the team safely through the gorge, but about 150 miles before the ghost town of Iditarod, where Doug plans to take his mandatory twenty-four-hour break, the team runs into trouble. A dusting of fresh snow hides the overflow of a small tributary. Elmer crashes through the soft top layer of ice. With a splash, the rest of the team hits the water. The sled, in jeopardy, heads directly toward thin ice. Some of the dogs rear back as the cold water reaches their skin. But Elmer doesn't flinch. He pushes forward steadily, lifting his paws higher. Before Doug can yell, "Gee, Elmer, gee," meaning "turn right," his powerful lead dog has pulled his teammates in that direction, toward solid ground. Doug halts the team on fresh dry snow and disembarks to pat Elmer on the head. He looks him straight in the eye. "Good call, ol' boy," he says.

Now, with a good stretch still remaining before the halfway stopover, Doug performs a chore he'd hoped could wait. The dog's thin but durable fabric booties are soaking wet and starting to freeze. He removes them one by one to let the drier snow absorb the water in their paws. Then he diligently fits new booties on all sixty-four paws, remembering with a grimace the one thousand booties he sometimes uses in a single race.

On the trail again, bonded by the hardship and difficulties they have surmounted together, Elmer and the team run strong and tight. A raven glides gracefully overhead, in front of Elmer, and he leaps up after it without missing a beat. His antics energize the entire team and they pick up speed, chasing the flying black tease. Elmer runs, eyes glued to the bird, until the trickster hides in a tree. Elmer barks, a sound rarely heard from a running sled dog.

"You goofball, Elmer," Doug laughs, thinking it's his dog's playfulness that helps make him such a great lead. He can entertain himself and his teammates as they cover the long miles of sometimes monotonous terrain. "He never gets bored. He just has a great sense of humor."

At Iditarod, far off the beaten path, Doug breaks out straw to bed down his dogs and then attends to Elmer. Years and immeasurable hours on the trail have created a special bond between him and his dog. Doug knows that Elmer is experienced enough to take full advantage of the rest periods. On the frequent stops along the trail to feed and check the dogs, and now on the twenty-four-hour break, Elmer conserves his energy. He lies down, nose tucked under his tail. His example spreads throughout the team. At home, Elmer might try to beat Doug to the couch, but in the Alaskan twilight it is Doug who lays his sleeping bag beside his team leader. Soon, human and dogs are fast asleep on the moon-dappled white blanket of snow.

From Iditarod, they are the first team to reach the Yukon River, which earns Doug $3,500 in cash and a seven-course gourmet meal at the Regal Alaskan Hotel. He's thinking about the scrumptious feast as the wind picks up and the temperature drops.

He feels the brutal cold coming at him. It bites like razor-sharp teeth through gaps in his clothing, where mittens join parka and where boots meet pants.

The team, led by Stormy, runs along the Yukon River, just a few hours ahead of the second-place dogsled. Elmer "rests" in the swing position.

It starts to blow. It's a wind Doug can hear and see—a wind that, despite his six years racing in the north, he has only heard of, but knows enough to fear.

The team runs full-out in the middle of the river, exposed, avoiding the deep snow on the banks. In some places, the river is half a mile wide, and the wind whips up the snow from all sides like a savage inferno. They are caught in the nightmare of all northern explorers—a whiteout. Doug can't tell where the trail is. He has heard of travelers losing their bearings and perishing on the windswept ice. The lead dog, Stormy, begins to pull toward the bank, unable to make out the trail.

"Whoa," Doug cries out from the relative shelter of the shore.

Intimidated by the howling blizzard, the dogs pile to a halt. Knowing his dogs need sustenance, Doug breaks out his frozen meat. As the dogs eat, he checks their feet, making sure their leather booties are securely attached.

The musher stands by his team, looking out into nothingness. All the dogs have lain down and curled into tight balls, using the snow as their blanket. All except one. Elmer sits upright beside Doug as if to say, "C'mon, boss, we can do it." Somewhere on the river lies the trail, but the wind has worsened. Doug knows that if any dog can face that wind it's Elmer. If they brave

the storm and push on, they will win the race. If they stay put, another team could pass them and they'd never even know.

Doug unhooks Elmer's harness and reattaches him to the lead. Elmer strains mightily, raising the other dogs. The tow rope is taut. Doug barely has time to haul up the snow anchor and yell, "All right, let's go," before the sled explodes straight out into the drifting snow.

Despite the wind, Elmer's excitement feeds the other dogs and their combined muscle transfers energy through the lines, developing power and speed. Doug fastens his goggles and tightens his fur hood. The team and the race are now Elmer's responsibility. Without hesitation, the superb athlete confidently leads the team back out along the river into the blinding white maelstrom.

Elmer surges forward with Doug holding on in the rear. In the chaos of wind and snow, Doug cannot make himself heard. More than ever, his survival depends on the understanding and trust between him and his dog.

An hour out along the river, the gale intensifies. The wind chill drives the temperature below minus sixty degrees Fahrenheit. A white hurricane totally envelops the team. Doug tightens his face muffler and leans forward, desperately hanging on to the sled. He believes in Elmer. Their bond grows stronger with each difficult situation and this is the toughest one they've ever faced.

Elmer leads the team unerringly along the 22 Mile Bend trail, and only when the sled starts drifting toward the bank does Doug realize they've reached Kaltag, the end of the river trail. "I could bear hug that dog," he sighs in relief. He bends down and squeezes Elmer hard around his furry neck, embracing the vital force of his sinewy lead dog. Thanks to Elmer's courageous deed, the team has a commanding ten-and-a-half-hour lead. With only 360 miles left to Nome, Doug Swingley can almost taste his second Itidarod win.

As they head up over the Kaltag portage and down to Unalakleet, Doug has time to think about Elmer's incredible strength and determination. Pulling through the whiteout was akin to the historical feats performed by Togo and Balto. Later, he will learn that his team was the only one to mush on through the vicious blizzard. The ringing bells of the snow-covered church in Unalakleet interrupt his thoughts. In this isolated Inupiat village, winter is a difficult time, and the Iditarod is the bright light in a long, dark season. The villagers greet the team warmly, but after just a few hours to rest and eat, Doug and his dogs hit the trail for the final stretch to Nome.

Nine days after leaving Anchorage, Elmer victoriously leads his exhausted team through the burled spruce arch that marks the finish line of the 1999 Iditarod. Hundreds of people swarm about, calling his name and reaching out

to touch the dog that so courageously led his team to a second Iditarod vic-
tory. He is voted the most outstanding lead dog by all the competing mushers
and awarded the coveted Golden Harness Award.

On the winner's podium beside Doug, Elmer hears the crowd's cheers
reach a crescendo. Doug waves jubilantly. Fame and prize money are his, but
Elmer deserves his fair share of the limelight. Doug steps back proudly to
allow the throng a better view of his champion sled dog. Elmer twists his
head—he doesn't care for the crowd's adulation, he's looking for his friend.
Doug bends down to reassure him, "forever grateful to this incredible dog
who never once let me down." Side by side with his master, a garland of yellow roses replacing the harness around his neck, Elmer turns to Doug and
licks his face. Camera shutters click and flashbulbs explode, forever immor-
talizing man and dog's triumphant conquest over hostile elements in the Iditarod, the last great race on earth.

PART FIVE

SERVICE DOGS

ENDAL

Endal picks up bread, milk, and cereal, loads them into the shopping basket, puts the wallet in the cashier's tray, scoops up the change, and follows his friend Allen's wheelchair out the door. At the first intersection, Endal stops, presses the pedestrian crossing button, and reminds his buddy to look both ways before advancing, something Allen Parton often forgets because of his memory loss. Miscalculating the proximity of an oncoming car, Allen starts forward and Endal blocks his way until it's safe to cross.

Acquaintances hail them as they wheel through Clanfield village, and Allen can't remember who they are. But Endal recognizes them all and his charming greetings prompt Allen to wish them a cheery hello. The couple moves smoothly through the streets, Endal eyeing the ladies, chatting up his mates, the perfect social buffer, icebreaker, and personal assistant par excellence.

Of course, the three-year-old yellow Labrador retriever has been groomed since infancy for this job.

Endal is a highly trained service dog, a Canine Partner for Independence, christened Endal because, as Allen wholeheartedly attests, "he's my be-all and end-all."

Endal's British-based Canine Partners for Independence (CPI) center has been active since 1990, although the potential of dogs to help the physically disabled was first realized in the United States in 1976. Labradors are the breed of choice for this work. They are sturdy and confident, and their eagerness to please, along with their forgiving disposition, greatly facilitates their training. Bred originally as a retriever for bird hunting, Labradors have strong fetching and carrying instincts. Their natural inclination to pick up objects and their gentle, cooperative nature make them ideal helpers for those who are disabled.

World-class dog trainer Nina Bondarenko, responsible for the selection and training of all CPI dogs, first tested Endal when he was seven weeks old. Before the assessment began, Nina established herself as his "master," staring at and not immediately touching Endal so he knew she was the "lead dog in the pack." Once the hierarchy in the relationship was established, Endal felt confident about learning from her.

The test could begin.

Nina lay Endal on his back in the garden and held him immobile. Rather than panic, struggle, or bite, as less calm puppies might do, Endal submitted quietly, gently licking Nina's hand.

She dropped a rolled sock near his face. Endal didn't chew it, run off with it, or hide it. In true retriever form, he picked up the sock and, as soon as Nina called, returned it to her, showing his desire to please.

Nina fired a starting pistol behind Endal's head. The startled puppy looked up at Nina, figured out she was the origin of the noise, and continued playing, maintaining his composure once again.

Endal's calmness, self-control, and good retrieving instincts assured Nina he had the potential to be an invaluable career service dog. Knowing seven-week-old puppies love their mother's touch, she scrunched up her new pupil's face in her hands, nibbled his ears, and rubbed his nose.

Once selected, Endal was assigned to a foster home for a year of basic training and socialization. His family of "puppy walkers" brought him everywhere, including train stations, football matches, shopping malls, wildlife preserves, and the hospital, where he was introduced to disinfectant smells and high-tech equipment he hadn't encountered before.

Every week, Endal attended puppy classes at the CPI training center in Petersfield, England, learning basic obedience and also to greet strangers with a paw shake, eliminate on command, call an elevator, load and empty the washer and dryer, fetch named items such as the newspaper and mail, carry whatever was required, and pick up everything dropped with or without command.

Over the following year, Endal became proficient in an astounding range of commands—ninety in all—standard training for a top CPI service dog.

A Four-Legged Person

Endal sleeps in luxury on deep quilts and soft bedding beside Allen's bed. He checks Allen throughout the night, touching him under the quilt "just to make sure I'm there." As day dawns, Endal senses a change in Allen's breathing and knows he will soon be awake. He greets him with excitement, tail wagging and banging against the wall, "as if we've not seen each other for seven whole hours even though we were inches apart." Impatient to begin the day, the yellow Lab jumps on Allen's bed and helps push his paralyzed legs over the side. He brings Allen his slippers, then trots to the bathroom, turns the doorknob

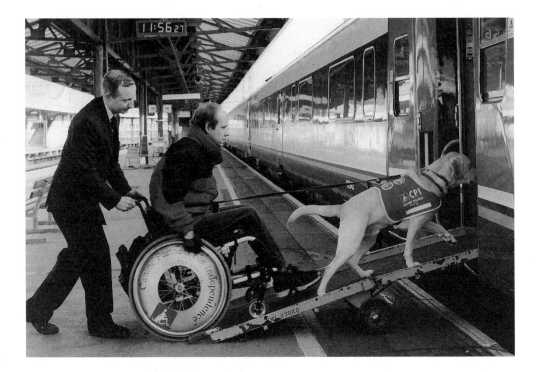

in his mouth, jumps up to hit the light switch with his paw, and considerately noses up the toilet seat. Allen finishes his ablutions and Endal, anticipating his needs, or noticing the stubble still on his face, fetches Allen's razor and drops it on his lap as if to say, "Here, make yourself presentable." Allen chuckles as he wheels out of the bathroom, noting once again that this typical male dog of his "lifts the seat but always forgets to put it down again."

Endal bounces downstairs for the meal his master has prepared the night before, returns the bowl, licked clean, lets himself out to the garden for his morning needs, and then tends to Allen.

He opens the high cupboard door, removes cereal, bowl, spoon, knife, fork, his gentle bird-dog mouth, apart from an occasional dribble, presenting all the items intact.

Discerning the delivery man's approach, Endal leaps off to fetch the newspaper and mail, capping his morning ministrations.

Energized by this love and devotion, Allen hugs Endal and slips out of his wheelchair. Allen's two children and wife emerge sleepily into the kitchen to find the two buddies rolling around on the floor, roughhousing and cuddling. Allen is careful not to shut his eyes during "fun time" with his dog. This would send Endal into panic mode, cueing a distinctive "I need help" bark to alert the neighbors. Instead, Endal play-barks and slathers Allen with doggie kisses. Hauling himself back into his chair, Allen realizes he's forgotten a basic clothing item and knows who, in his family, to ask for it.

"Socks," Allen says, and Endal gallops upstairs, opens the drawer, gets the socks, shuts the drawer, bounces down, and deposits them on Allen's lap. A sock drops from Allen's hand and Endal picks it up and happily gives it back to him. Allen drops it a second time and Endal picks it up and gives it back to him again. "Once, it was my wife, Sandra, who used to pick things up for me," Allen thinks as he smoothes his sock on, "and if I dropped it a second time she'd pick it up again but groan, and if I dropped it a third time, she'd say, 'I'll do it.' Endal will sit there all day waiting for me to drop something, only too pleased to get it for me. He just looks for things to do for me."

Sensing they're going out, Endal fetches his collar, leash, and red CPI jacket. He gently lifts Allen's legs back onto the wheelchair.

"Keys," Allen says, knowing Endal will remember where he's left them. "Mobile," he adds, and Endal trots off to get the keys and the cell phone, returning to place them in the carryall behind Allen's wheelchair.

Allen waves his family a cheery good-bye.

Then, fully prepared, the canine/human team wheels independently out the door en route to the CPI training center.

The hangar-like building, on the outskirts of a small village in Hampshire, is furnished with wheelchairs, a mock post office, a mural of an elevator with an active call button, supermarket shelves and a checkout, rows of washing machines, and a mock pedestrian crossing. Inside the homey living room, trainer Nina Bondarenko busily teaches a standard poodle to turn on the light, a plastic globe that illuminates when nudged. Using a wand, a fistful of doggie treats, and a clicker that signals a reward, Bondarenko encourages the poodle to butt the rod in her hand. Touch. "Good," she says, clicks and gives a treat. Nina holds the tip of the wand close to the globe, her hand covering its bottom half. With each nudge, the dog's nose gets closer to the end of the wand until he finally butts the light, not the wand. Click . . . "good dog" . . . treat. Within sixty seconds, the poodle has got the hang of it, and is switching the light on and off to order. He gulps down his treats.

Comfortably ensconced, Allen and Endal welcome a prospective service dog recipient. Allen explains to the wheelchair-bound woman that when the dog is ill, you have to look after it, you have to feed it. "The dog's not a robot. What you take from it you have to give back. It gives you love, you've got to love it back twice as hard; it works hard for you so you've got to let it play twice as hard." Allen caresses Endal's shiny golden coat and toned body, the dog's plumed tail beating a joyous accompaniment to his master's words.

Allen first came to the training center after three years in rehab and an additional year at home relearning how to talk, read, write, and think after a paralyzing Gulf War head injury. He figured he had lost sixty percent of his former emotional, intellectual, and physical self. Also, his memory was severely affected. He couldn't recall being married or the birth of his children. "My family's husband and dad had gone away and never come back, just this miserable chap in a wheelchair. For a long time, I was stuck at home doing nothing. I wouldn't talk to people; I wouldn't answer the phone; I was very insular. My family had carried me through so much of the rehab process, but in a sense I

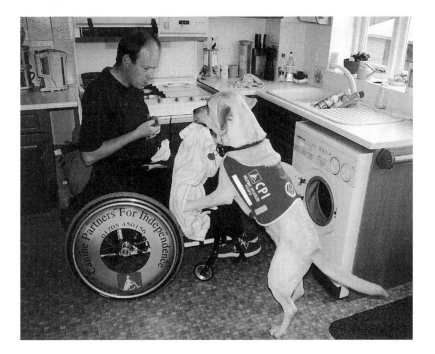

just didn't want to live anymore; I was just waiting for my time to come, in a funny sort of way."

Sandra, Allen's wife, decided she wanted to be a "puppy walker" and took Allen with her to the nearby CPI training center. He would go with her to the puppy classes and sit alone in a corner, shutting out the world. "But the dogs saw right through me. They came up to me and kept bugging me, nudging me, licking me, saying hello. Despite the fact that I was a big, hard, miserable chap in the corner, the dogs saw that I wasn't a bad person, I was just fairly mixed up and broken."

Endal, meanwhile, was living in the center full-time, perfecting his skills and having his response to commands fine-tuned. First the young pupil had to learn to follow Nina in the wheelchair. When Nina first moved the wheelchair backward a couple of feet, Endal looked at her, bemused, wondering what to do. He came around to the front and put his paw on Nina's knee. "No," Nina laughed. "Wrong choice; try again." She budged the wheelchair back a few more inches. This time, Endal followed closely, and Nina rewarded him. For the next half hour, caught up in the fun of Nina's "operant conditioning," reinforced with constant praise, encouragement, and games, the willing Labrador heeled happily, as Nina gradually increased the complexity of her wheelchair maneuvers. Endal was given tasks when he was judged ready and was rewarded for his success. "You watch the behavior the dog is offering and reward him for the behavior nearest to what you want," Nina explained to the puppy walkers. "As punishment, we withdraw attention, so the puppy learns you have lost interest in him. They'd rather be petted than ignored."

Endal was never forced to do a task or punished, as was often the case with the older, harsher dog training methods. Constantly challenged with "Here's a problem, solve it," Endal developed the creativity and flexibility to respond to Allen's needs. He drove his own training, which was interspersed with runs, walks, and play time, giving him plenty of space to just be himself.

When Endal first met Allen, he and the other dogs immediately sensed the difference between their able-bodied trainers in wheelchairs and the man alone in the corner. Endal nudged Allen, moving carefully and gently around his legs.

"The dogs kept coming up to me and even when I pushed them away, they kept coming back. And finally I was talking to them, laughing. I mean, when I came back from the Gulf, I didn't know happiness, sadness, love, hate. I didn't have any of these feelings. But these dogs were getting things out of me no one else had. And one of these dogs, Endal, who is my baby, kept pursuing that, and kept working at me and nudging at me."

Bit by bit, the CPI staff involved Allen in helping them train the dogs to maneuver by the side of a wheelchair. Next they asked him to take the more advanced dogs outside to further hone their wheelchair skills. Allen's feeling of self-worth hit an all-time high. "I was actually helping other people!"

And then the charity asked Allen if he would like to apply for a dog.

For Allen, making the application was another nail in his coffin, another badge of disability he didn't want to accept.

"From the Gulf War to then, I'd never admitted I had a disability. Doing the application was a psychological boost for me, because if you admit something, you can do something about it."

Together, Endal and Allen undertook the strenuous two-week residential training course and passed the final Marks & Spencer department store shopping test with flying colors, "since Endal knew everything anyway. It was the chap in the wheelchair who didn't have a clue."

Now Allen answers the phone at the center, organizes training outings for CPI owners and dogs, does demos with Endal, and continues to help other people. Last month, Endal and Allen tackled the problem of how to ensure aid for people who fall unconscious from their wheelchairs without having time to press the alarms around their necks. They devised a telephone unit with a red emergency alert button that buzzes when pressed. With the buzzing as their reward, Endal and the other dogs learned to target the red button as well as bark when someone simulated falling unconscious from his or her chair. Soon after this system was devised, a CPI dog used this training to save his master's life. Endal was just the medicine Allen needed to start communicating again. "My family had lovingly carried me so far, but Endal carried me that bit farther. He doesn't judge me, he doesn't look away from my condition, and he makes me laugh, the world's best cure."

As Allen and Endal wheel through Clanfield, villagers stop them to ask, "How's Endal; what's his latest exploit?" making the outing longer and much more enjoyable than before, when Allen, mired in isolated misery, spoke to no one. They approach the bank and Endal soon hears the beep of the automatic teller machine. Allen feels his dog's excitement through the lead. Endal eagerly grabs the money out of the slot and gives it to Allen, "the only trouble being, when he sees other people at the machine, he's just as enthusiastic about taking their money, giving new meaning to charitable street collection."

In the shops without wheelchair access, Endal takes Allen's wallet and a message in his mouth, bounces up the steps, delivers them to the counter, and brings back the wallet with Allen's purchase.

Innocently jumping the long lottery line, to the surprise and delight of those waiting, Endal buys Allen's lottery ticket.

In the supermarket, the helpful yellow Lab retrieves canned soup and a bag of apples from the shelves and, in mid-aisle, impulsively pulls his toy Kong from Allen's bag, playfully tearing up and down the waxed floors with it, slipping and sliding, four legs in every direction. Allen bursts out laughing and a grinning shopper says it's the first time she's ever heard laughter in a supermarket. "Dogs don't have a work ethic," Allen remembers Nina saying.

"They don't believe that they have to be on duty and later they can relax. They are relaxed all the time and, equally, aware all the time."

"It isn't an issue," Allen agrees. "That's just Endal. It's his nature."

At the pub, Endal heads straight for the bar, puts his front paws on the counter, and deposits Allen's wallet, barking to attract the bar staff. Allen orders a drink and chips, and Endal collects the wallet and change. Nearby, a tipsy patron rubs his eyes in utter amazement. "Did I just see a dog buy a drink?"

But the real challenge of the day, the appointment Allen nervously anticipates, is the scheduled visit to his daughter's school to demonstrate what Endal can do, an invitation Allen considers "the nicest acceptance of me by my children." When Allen came home after the Gulf War, Zoe, then eleven years old, couldn't stand the pressure and packed herself off to boarding school. Liam, at twelve, felt much the same way but didn't want to leave home. "Now the children have seen me mellow out with time, even get silly with the dog, dropping my guard a little. Every day, a nicer side of me is revealed, Endal carefully dragging it out of me. I love my children so much but I've been inhibited in showing it to them. I'm not sure how, but Endal aids in the process. Both children asked me to speak at their schools and I think they must be accepting the new fellow that's come home now."

Rows of expectant young faces, including Allen's daughter, watch Endal going through his paces, a sampling of the awesome skills of a highly trained service dog. Allen had worried he'd stutter and mix up words, causing Zoe's friends to make fun of her. Now, seeing the students' rapt attention, father and daughter exchange a complicit smile.

"Some days, Endal will do less because he knows I'm quite fit that day," Allen says. "And then the next day, if I'm stiff and having a bad day, he offers me more. He knows. The other day I dropped a big grocery bag in the kitchen. He knew I could reach it and didn't get off his bed, and I thought, 'Right, you little sausage, I'll drop something I can't reach,' and I dropped a bluntish knife. He came and picked that up and I dropped something else I could pick up, and he left it. He was determining what I could and couldn't do. 'I'm not making him lazy, he can get that himself,' Endal figured, offering up the behavior he thought was appropriate. My dog's not a slave, but when I need help, he's always there."

"What's the most clever thing Endal does?" asks one of Zoe's friends.

"Knowing what I need," Allen answers after a moment's hesitation. "It's like having that extra brainpower where mine doesn't work. Endal has perceived it and he just offers it up. It's like putting oil on a stuck mechanism. It just oils the day."

Allen's heart fills with joy as Zoe stands proudly near him. For this occasion, he had really focused and it seems everything went well. "I don't think I let her down." As the students mill enthusiastically around the inspiring visitors, Allen confidently looks forward to their next challenge—the demo at Liam's school.

On the way home, Allen powers off-road in his supercharged, all-terrain wheelchair. Endal bounds ecstatically ahead in the woods, both letting off steam during their daily half hour of let-rip dog time. "Whatever he wants— tuggie games with a Kong, sniffing around finding hidden things, playing, just being a dog."

They relax at home after dinner, Endal following Allen everywhere, trained to open doors even when Allen shuts them, "so he goes wherever he likes." Allen's family gathers in the living room, and Endal gets the cuddles he loves. He climbs on the sofa to be close to Allen, "always touching me in some way, even if it is just his head on my footrest." By the end of the evening, Endal has taken over the sofa and the family's seated on the floor. No one

cares because Endal has helped Allen overcome the bitterness he felt about his disability and has made all their lives so much better. Allen knows he will always have a memory problem, but every day, hour, and minute remind him that "having someone with you twenty-four hours a day who loves you unconditionally makes you feel good about yourself. Endal's my four-legged friend, my lifesaver, my mate. I love him to bits."

CAYENNE

Shiny, black Cayenne and her four kennel mates are shoved pell-mell into a homey, compact recreation room. Already, the room is teeming with kids and dogs. The sounds of laughter, shrieks, and excited barking fill the air. Cayenne looks around, bemused, adjusting to her surroundings. After six months of intense training, this spontaneous mayhem is too much fun.

Which of the seven giggling, joyous kids should she go to first?

A slight, dark-haired eleven-year-old attracts Cayenne's attention. She seems peaceful and relaxed. Cayenne makes a beeline for Esther and launches herself onto her lap. Cooing with pleasure, Esther runs her hands over Cayenne's body. She feels the softness of the warm, furry animal, traces the contours of her gentle head with her fingertips, finds and strokes the silkiness of her ears.

Cayenne snuggles into Esther, both dog and child closing their eyes in contentment. When they open their eyes, only one of them is able to see the bustle of kids and dogs playing around them. But, now, the sighted dog and the blind child can safely navigate the melee and begin their life together.

Esther has found her seeing-eye guide to the world, and Cayenne has found her reason to live.

From this moment on, Cayenne will be at Esther's side.

Cayenne, a four-year-old "Labernese," is the brainchild of Eric St. Pierre. A Labernese is an inspired cross between the Bernese mountain dog, bred to herd and guard cattle in the Alps near Bern, and the Labrador retriever, bred to hunt waterfowl. St. Pierre is the founder of the MIRA Foundation, a guide and service-dog training center in Quebec, Canada, devoted to enhancing the functional capabilities of handicapped people. He worked a long time with purebred dogs like the Bernese mountain dog and the Labrador before creating this new breed, "the first highly sociable breed created by mankind," he says proudly, "with the unique goal of serving the handicapped." Cayenne is also the first dog in North America to guide a child as young as eleven, Esther's age when she first met and fell in love with her dog.

In the furry black, white, and tan Bernese mountain dog, St. Pierre found a strong instinct for loyalty and the desire to protect. He was also impressed by their amazing capacity to understand and analyze complex situations. The problem, however, was their extreme intelligence and sensitivity. Bernese mountain dogs don't suffer human error or scolding easily, and can sulk and hold grudges.

For St. Pierre's purposes, the strong, beautiful Labrador retriever, "graced with an infinite sense of forgiveness," was the perfect complement to the Bernese mountain dog. The Lab has a joyful, highly sociable disposition. Even when owners give dangerous commands, or ask the impossible, then punish them for disobeying orders, Labs instantly forgive and regain their bright disposition at the first loving gesture. The main drawback St. Pierre found in Labradors was that their hunting instinct, combined with their confident love of all people, could lead them to wander away from their owners when off duty.

So St. Pierre crossed the intelligent, intensely loyal Bernese with the strong, good-natured Labrador, creating a wonderful communication medium for integrating the blind and disabled into society, the Labernese.

Thus, loyal, protective, gentle, sensitive, unshakable Cayenne was born.

Best Friends

Cayenne springs to attention as Esther unhooks the dog's solid metal-and-leather harness and shakes it briskly. Cayenne thrusts her furry head into the self-supporting apparatus, chest firmly against the strap. Esther reaches around her dog's belly and buckles her in. The sixty-pound Labernese has been anticipating this moment since dawn. Although Esther can easily navigate the familiar obstacles of her two-bedroom family apartment, once out the door she needs Cayenne's guidance and reassuring presence to get to school. Cayenne's inherited instincts to love and please Esther were reinforced, starting almost at birth, by training. After two months of puppy bliss, chewing, playing, sleeping, and eating with her mother and littermates in the MIRA maternity wing, Cayenne began socialization with her foster family—malls, restaurants, strangers, buses—relaxing and enjoying people. At eighteen months of age, she said good-bye to her foster family and returned to MIRA for an intensive six-month course in guide-dog training.

Esther pats Cayenne affectionately on the head and ruffles her ears.

Out the front door, down five steps, left turn onto the street. Immediately, Cayenne's determined pace falters. Left turn means school, and she'd rather go anywhere else than wait long hours under a desk. Esther has to pull her reluctant dog down the first block before Cayenne's sense of duty kicks in and she assumes her proper position, left and front, tail brushing Esther's knee.

Esther applies pressure on the harness so she can feel Cayenne leading her. Her left hand is her sensor, her antenna. All changes in direction are communicated to Esther through the handle, a sort of interface that transmits data on the direction to follow. With just the right amount of pressure, Esther can keep close contact with her dog, feeling Cayenne guide her around obstacles. Holding the handle too tightly, she would miss Cayenne's signals and also interfere with her dog's movements. Holding it too loosely, she could drop her lifeline. Like a rider holding the reins of his horse, or a dancer following

her partner, Esther flows with Cayenne's every subtle move. Cayenne leads with a sure, confident pace.

Initially sad and lonely when she left her foster family to start training at MIRA, Cayenne quickly adapted to her new kennel mates and learned to love and respect her firm but affectionate trainer, Karen Winters. She passed a battery of physical exams and laboratory tests—fecal analysis, heartworm testing, complete blood count, biochemical profile, X-rays for hip dysplasia—and also psychological tests evaluating her character and reaction to cats, noises, playing dogs, pack behavior, dominance, and submission. In her first month, she was trained to stay in her run with the door open unless otherwise instructed, to guide Karen forward and around ninety-degree turns, and to submit to pulling, poking, and prodding of her ears, legs, and whole body. Constantly reinforced with praise and food, Cayenne learned to adjust her stride to avoid unbalancing her handler, avoid fixed or moving objects, evaluate the distance above and around herself and her trainer, and protect her handler by refusing an order when the order put them at risk. Intelligent, sweet-natured Cayenne blossomed in the warmhearted learning environment, developing self-confidence, trust in human beings, and a profound love of her work. By her third month of training, Cayenne could lead blindfolded Karen through an obstacle course, up and down steps, around fire hydrants, and across quiet streets.

Walking at a quick, sure pace, the team hits the first, quiet street crossing. Cayenne stops. Esther pats her head and feels the curb with her toe, gauging the sound of the cars.

"Forward," Esther commands, sensing all is clear.

Down the curb, following the dip of the harness, across the street, stopping at the curb, stepping up with the rise of the harness, Esther and Cayenne safely navigate the first crossing of their regular, practiced route.

Then four more blocks and a ninety-degree left turn past the sound of kids playing in her old grade school. With only ten minutes left, they detour wide around a puddle and past two playful puppies that Cayenne ignores. Three more brisk blocks and they've reached the biggest challenge of their route.

They stop, facing a five-lane intersection at rush hour. Cars are honking, humming, and merging from all directions.

Before Cayenne, this busy intersection would have been a dangerous nightmare for Esther. She pats the top of Cayenne's head, remembering life before she got her dog. "I was unable to do much alone, not getting out much unless someone was always around me, growing older but always feeling like a baby."

Meeting two-year-old Cayenne was Esther's ultimate payoff after her own spatial orientation and mobility training. During the course of a month at MIRA, with other visually impaired children and teenagers, Esther and Cayenne began to weave the private bond that so intimately unites them.

Esther listens vigilantly to the traffic patterns, slim body erect, face toward the street, focused on the sounds revealing the direction of the rushing cars. Cayenne, a blaze of white on her black chest and distinctive white hairs on her nose and muzzle, stands calmly beside her, a deceptive look of concentration on her face. Cayenne isn't studying traffic lights or rushing cars to decide when to cross the street. She is awaiting orders from her boss. In this team, work and responsibility is shared equally. Esther decides when to cross but Cayenne intervenes if necessary. Should a car veer toward Esther, or stop in her path, it's Cayenne's responsibility to quickly move her out of harm's way.

If Esther and Cayenne combine their skill and training, they can safely cross to the other side.

Hearing the cars stop parallel to her, Esther knows her light is red and she must wait. This intersection is so dangerous that the city has installed a sound device on the traffic light that chirps an auditory signal when the lights change. Esther remembers the many days spent practicing with her instructor, painstakingly creating detailed mental images of the city routes she would travel with Cayenne. She used to stand at this light a long time before she would cross.

"When to decide to go, that's the hardest part."

The parallel traffic moves, the audio signal chirps, and Esther hears the light is green. She feels safe with Cayenne, knowing her dog is devoted to her, would do anything for her, even protect her with her life. She can cross.

"Forward," she tells Cayenne decisively.

Immediately, the harness dips down off the curb, and girl and dog walk briskly across the major intersection as if it's the easiest thing in the world.

"*Bon chien,* good dog," says Esther, using the French praise words she learned at MIRA.

Cayenne's wagging tail acknowledges her pleasure at doing her job and serving her mistress well.

Inside her high school, Esther rewards Cayenne with a delicious end-of-walk treat and takes her by the leash instead of the harness, so Cayenne won't get pushed and will have more leeway to navigate the halls.

"Locker," Esther commands, using one of the new words, like "subway," and "bus," she has taught Cayenne. The smart black dog faithfully leads Esther through hundreds of talking, jostling, socializing teenagers, directly to her locker to meet Claire and Kirsty, her closest friends. They load up Esther's extra books and her Brailler, a ten-pound scanning device that converts the written word to Braille. Cayenne waits contentedly, enjoying Esther's laughter, happy when Esther is happy, sad when Esther is sad.

Once in the familiar corridor, Cayenne leads Esther toward her first class. Of the many corridors and staircases in the school, Cayenne and Esther know only the routes to each class. Kids bustling to beat the bell block their path. Confused, Cayenne waits for the crowd to thin and Esther, late for class, reassures her and figures out the direction to take. "C'mon, girl, let's go right."

Esther applies herself to the morning routine and Cayenne endures it— math class under the desk, brief break, a minute of glorious walking, English under the desk, brief break, forty-five minutes of geography.

By the time the lunch bell rings, the normally quiet, calm dog is restless with pent-up energy.

She fidgets from paw to paw.

"Outside," Esther commands, patting her head in sympathy, and Cayenne leads her quickly outside.

"Water," Esther commands, and Cayenne leads her to the drinking fountain in the field behind the school. Cayenne drinks the overflow, slurps, licks her mistress all over, and then guides Esther to her ultimate destination, the picnic table beside the fountain, where her friends wait.

"Without Cayenne, I couldn't have found the picnic table. It's far off, three to five minutes away. I would have never known what direction it is. Once we're in the field, Cayenne knows where the water fountain is and the picnic table too. I don't eat lunch alone anymore."

Happily ensconced between Claire and Kirsty, Esther removes Cayenne's harness to let her relax. Joking, she flaps Cayenne's ears up and down, then holds them up, "like a German shepherd's ears," for all to see. Off duty, Cayenne shakes, rolls in the grass, bounds exuberantly around the girls, barking, growling, inviting them to play. Normally, the girls would happily respond, but today, being Friday, they have arrangements to discuss—science assignment, Saturday's study schedule, Sunday horseback riding.

"I didn't have friends two years ago. If I did, they were visually impaired, like me. Now Kirsty, Claire, and I go swimming and horseback riding together. They started wanting to be my friends because they liked Cayenne, and I let them pat her and play with her. Now we all understand each other. They have the same feelings I have about things."

Claire and Kirsty have asked to keep Cayenne when Esther gets a new guide dog and Cayenne retires. If Esther's apartment can hold both the new dog and Cayenne, Esther would prefer to keep her. If not, when faced with this decision in six years, at least she's assured that her friends will love Cayenne and care for her.

Cayenne lays her head on Esther's lap while the girls talk and giggle. Almost reflexively, Esther's hands drift to Cayenne's ears. She massages the margins, strokes the silky parts, kneading her dog's ears. Cayenne closes her eyes, lost in the private ritual of their shared caress.

The end-of-lunch bell signals Esther's favorite, most active class and Cayenne's most upsetting school experience—gym. Cayenne used to attend gym, but the sight of her mistress running and roughhousing with classmates worried Cayenne. She barked, concerned that Esther was being hurt, and jumped on her, trying to protect her. Now Cayenne has to wait for Esther in the vice-principal's office.

Tail between her legs, head slumped on her front paws, eyes on the door, ears cocked for Esther's return, Cayenne mopes. Without Esther, she is lost and sad. She sighs unhappily, anxious and uneasy at the separation from her beloved companion. The hour-long gym class seems interminable until she recognizes Esther's distant footsteps. Slowly, her tail begins to wag and she jumps up to stand at the door. Showering her mistress with kisses, offering first her right and then her left paw, "tail wagging so fast that whatever it hits she doesn't care," Cayenne buries her head deep into Esther's body. Esther laughs happily at her best friend's antics.

"Home," says Esther when the school day ends, and Cayenne willingly and confidently leads Esther directly back, safely home.

Now it's Esther's turn to look after Cayenne, the sacred after-school time that Cayenne loves best. Basking in Esther's undivided attention, she soaks up her ministrations. First a thorough grooming, then ear cleaning and a nail clip, followed by a brushing of her pearly whites with a specially formulated, delicious, enzymatic chicken toothpaste. Health and beauty assured, it's time for Cayenne's favorite game, tiger tug, with Esther astride her stuffed tiger and Cayenne excitedly barking, growling, digging, and pulling it out from under her.

Outside, their play takes flight. Esther chases the elusive Cayenne, whom she can never catch. Then she hides so Cayenne can find her. Each time Cayenne discovers Esther hidden under the deck, or behind the backyard bush, she is just as ecstatic, her joy at their reunion just as genuine and miraculous, as all the other times before. And every time she is found, Esther embraces and praises her wondrous, playful Labernese guide dog, her other half, who "makes me feel like a real person," and has brought hope and independence to her life.

. . . .

MICHIGAN, U.S.A.

WILLIE

Joanne leaves Willie, her red-coated golden retriever, on the shore, and positions herself at the end of the pier. It's a hot July afternoon at Dog Scout camp, and men, women, children, and dogs of all shapes, colors, and sizes are swimming in the lake, sunning on the pebbly beach, or snoozing in the shade. Willie watches his sweet-faced blond mistress raise her camera, adjust the focus, and place her finger on the button to photograph the idyllic scene.

Then, like a thrown switch, something in Willie clicks.

He leaps to his feet and races toward Joanne, barking frantically.

Joanne heeds her dog's warning and lowers her camera. Willie nudges her insistently away from the edge of the pier. She heads quickly for solid ground. After five years together, she understands what he is signaling.

Within seconds, Joanne feels the strange aura, with its "sort of oniony smell," that precedes a grand mal seizure. The world begins to stretch and contract as if it's made of soft rubber, and Joanne collapses, unconscious.

. . .

Willie's special talent in predicting the onset of Joanne's epileptic seizures is one of the rarest, most mysterious canine gifts to humanity. Even in the specialized world of seizure dogs, trained to protect and help their epileptic owners, few possess Willie's uncanny ability to predict the onset of seizures. For Joanne, her dog's warnings mean the difference between a life of fearful worry and one of relative peace of mind.

At eight months of age, Willie received his basic training at Paws with a Cause in Wayland, Michigan, the largest service-dog training school in the United States. PAWS trains guide dogs, hearing dogs, mobility assistance dogs, emergency service dogs, and seizure dogs. Golden retrievers like Willie are a popular choice as a service dog. They were first bred in the British Isles in 1868 by Lord Tweedmouth, who crossed a Tweed water spaniel with a wavy-coated yellow retriever in an attempt to develop the perfect hunting dog. Further breeding over successive generations resulted in a water-loving golden retriever, which proved itself an excellent sporting dog, powerful and athletic, sound and well balanced. The breed's physical strengths and retrieving instincts, along with its sociability, self-confidence, and desire to please, are attributes inherent in Willie's gentle nature.

Michael Sapp, chief operating officer of Paws with a Cause, says it takes a special kind of animal to work as a seizure dog. Only two percent of the five hundred dogs tested so far have the necessary qualities of intelligence, patience, and gentleness required for seizure dog training. At PAWS, Willie learned to remove people with epilepsy from dangerous places at the onset of a seizure, and to protect them from harm while they were incapacitated. He was trained to operate emergency call devices for outside help, and respond to a buzzer, reminding his owner to take required medications. This training is vital to Joanne, because several times a day she has small petit mal seizures and blanks out briefly. With her conscious mind shut down, she might miss the buzzer and forget her medicine, thus precipitating a more severe grand mal seizure.

Of the twenty-eight seizure dogs trained at PAWS, only five showed Willie's remarkable ability to alert their owners to impending seizures. How they do it is still a mystery. Some researchers speculate that these dogs pick up a scent from the change in brain chemistry that accompanies a seizure. Or perhaps they detect tiny preseizure variants in the nervous system, like the seismic tremors that signal an earthquake. Whatever it is, the dogs that develop the talent do so only after spending years living with and caring for their owners. Their lifesaving seizure alerts are a wonder unequaled by human science. Before Willie arrived from Paws with a Cause, Joanne remembers a life filled with "fear and isolation." Going out alone with the specter of a grand mal seizure was potentially dangerous. People with epilepsy had been injured blacking out on busy streets. Some had awakened in hospitals listed as John or Jane Doe, robbed of all their identification and money. Joanne herself was once mugged while unconscious. Even in the relative security of her home during severe seizures, she was unable to summon help.

Now, Willie warns Joanne of impending seizures and protects her from harm, inside and out. When Joanne doesn't regain consciousness quickly enough after a seizure, he operates the footpad telephone her father built to call for help. "Willie," she says, "has given me my life back."

Because of his talent and unyielding devotion, Willie was named the Therapy Companion Animal of the Year by the Michigan Veterinary Medical Association. But in describing her six-year-old golden retriever, Joanne Weber uses much more personal terms: "Willie," she says, "is my savior."

On Call

Joanne wakes early to the chatter of chickadees outside the cabin window. She raises her sleepy head and sees Willie by the door, looking at her imploringly. Dog Scout camp shouldn't be wasted, his look implies. Let's get into the great outdoors.

The morning sun burnishes Willie's deep reddish fur to a golden hue as they amble down to the lake for a game of catch. Fellow campers poke their heads out of their rustic cabins, wave, and call greetings to Willie, as Joanne's artist's eye notes the play of light on his coat. She pats her dog's silky back. Knowing his mistress is safely surrounded by Dog Scout camp friends, Willie bounds ahead, only occasionally looking back.

Joanne watches the freedom of his movements, pleased to see her very responsible companion letting loose and enjoying camp. That's why she comes here—to join Willie in learning skills like flyball, backpacking, water rescue, Frisbee, search and rescue, and tracking, and to hear lectures on flora and fauna, wolf behavior, first aid, dog massage, and canine conditioning. But really, she comes so Willie can have fun with other dogs and relax.

They join a dozen happily chatting, sniffing dogs and people at a back-packing trail near the woods. The dogs, ranging from a small spaniel to a large Newfoundland, wear backpacks containing water bottles, bowls, flashlights, compasses, first-aid kits, pocketknives, extra leashes and collars, and, of course, pooper-scoopers. The morning's hike is a five-miler through the forested hills. The training purpose of the hike is to build up and maintain the dog's conditioning, especially necessary for service dogs like Willie, who tote their owners' valuables and medications wherever they go. The camp's motto for dogs is "Let us learn new things, that we may become more helpful," and the motto for their owners is "Our dogs' lives are much shorter than our own, so let's help them enjoy their time with us as much as we can." But the real reward for the dogs is simply a great walk in the woods in the company of their owners and a pack of canine playmates.

The group strolls at an easy pace, giving the dogs time to explore. Even on these camp hikes, Willie feels obliged to remain on call. He is far up the

trail when he hears the sound of Joanne's buzzer, but his reaction is immediate. He wheels around and bounds toward her with his alarm bark. "It's okay, Willie," she reassures him as she takes her medication. "Go have some fun."

The dog and human hikers climb to the peak of the hillside overlooking the lake and the camp

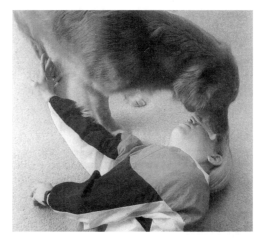

below. Satisfied that Joanne has taken her medication, Willie and a frisky cocker spaniel circle a chattering treed squirrel, their faces marked by the indignant look dogs get when confronted by small, noisy, inaccessible rodents. Finally, they give up, moving on to easier prey—a birch branch at the base of the tree. Willie, the retriever, happily grasps the wood treasure in his mouth, prances and dances around the scampering spaniel, shakes the stick vigorously, flips it in the air, and pounces before it hits the ground.

Lonnie Olson founded the Dog Scouts of America camp when she saw the sheer joy in her Border collie's eyes as he played on the lakeshore with other dogs. The only existing camps she knew focused on formal obedience, and she envisaged a more playful learning experience. Joanne knows this camp was conceived for dogs, but she admits she has come to enjoy these camp weeks as much as Willie does.

Two hours later, the weary and relaxed hiking crew arrives back at the camp for water rescue training. The heat has been building all morning and people and dogs jump gratefully into the refreshing lake to practice lifesaving. Willie fetches Joanne a life jacket, then a rescue rope, and, finally, himself as a furry flotation device. Joanne clutches his back, feeling the water eddy around her body, laughing to see the lake churning with lifesaving dogs and because she feels so good. Willie pulls her safely to shore. Then he shakes great arcs of spray over everyone and bounds back into the shallows, a true water-loving retriever.

Joanne's dog painting class begins soon after lunch. The Dog Scout campers are fitted with sponge booties dipped in nontoxic water-soluble paint, and the room gears up for a wildly hilarious art session. Owners hold up cardboard canvases and move them around while the dogs happily flail away, getting half the paint on the cardboard canvas and half on themselves and their laughing masters. After each successful swipe, the dogs are given a treat, which encourages their artistic endeavors. Willie has more practice than the others, since his painting lessons began in Joanne's studio, where she noticed Willie's curiosity about her painting. Willie already knew how to "wave," or lift his paw in the air. It was a short step from there to taping a paintbrush to his paw, holding up a piece of cardboard, and letting him go at it. Now, Willie is something of an expert, and his paintings are auctioned off at charity fund-raisers. Willie whacks the canvas with a gleeful look in Joanne's direction. It is one of his habits to look directly at her, eye to eye. "You're a good boy, Willie," she says. His wonderful red coat is speckled with green and yellow paint and he sports what looks very much like a grin on his face.

Before supper, everyone heads back to the lake for a final swim and to wash off the body paint. Joanne carries her camera to record the beach scene as a memento. Willie waits dutifully on shore, watching her walk to the end of the pier. She adjusts the focus and clearly sees her fellow campers scrubbing off paint and Willie, stretched out comfortably on the beach, gazing back at her through the lens.

Suddenly, Willie's entire demeanor undergoes a dramatic shift. He senses in Joanne an intangible signal so slight that only he, in all the world, can perceive it. He takes off toward Joanne like a shot, barking as if his lungs will burst, pleading with her to get off the dock before the seizure strikes.

When Joanne first hears him, she is surprised by the warning because she can honestly say, at that moment, surrounded by friends on this beautiful July afternoon, she has never felt better. But then comes the smell of onions, and the world begins to pitch and weave. She makes it to solid ground and settles in, still conscious, but her brain has lost control of her limbs and speech. The seizure builds inexorably toward its height. There is a pulsing strobe effect, without the light. Electrical impulses fire wildly in her brain, and she convulses helplessly on the ground. Gradually, she loses consciousness.

The last thing she sees is Willie standing over her, his eyes dark with concern, protecting her with his body. Then there is nothing.

Willie hovers over her. As always, he tries to revive her by licking her face. Joanne's friends crowd around, grateful to Willie for averting potential danger. If the seizure had struck unexpectedly, Joanne might have pitched into the water, hit her head, and drowned.

Finally, Joanne opens her eyes. The first thing she sees is Willie, her friend and protector, looking anxious. He is waiting for her to say the reassuring words, "I'm okay, Willie, I'm okay."

Back in their condo in Grand Blanc, Michigan, Willie settles into his favorite place. From the settee beside the studio window, he keeps an ear cocked for Joanne and checks to make sure all is well in the outside world. Joanne is immersed in fine-tuning an illustration program on her computer. Because her seizures are made much worse by stress, she avoids high-pressure commercial deadlines, but enjoys a wide range of graphic and fine-arts work. Willie recognizes an elderly couple from next door and gives them a wag. A squirrel scampers across the lawn and his face looks momentarily indignant. But he doesn't bark. That's saved for when it matters.

When Joanne takes a break to do laundry, Willie scampers down to be by her side. She recently had back surgery and has trouble lifting the hamper. With no prompting, Willie drags the hamper from her bedroom to the laundry room. He is halfway down the hall when the phone rings. He stops and looks at Joanne with a "You-want-me-to-get-it?" look.

Joanne smiles. "It's okay, Willie," she says. "I'll get it." Willie can fetch the portable phone and often does, but she worries sometimes that Willie is too devoted, too responsible. That's the beauty of Dog Scout camp, she thinks—hikes, water, play, some fun in Willie's life.

The buzzer goes off and Willie barks his medication bark, not letting up until he sees Joanne take her pills. Then he's quiet. The golden dog stretches out on his back on the settee, all four paws in the air, head upside down, mouth drooping, and long tongue hanging out. Joanne glances up from her computer and smiles. Sensing her looking at him, the upside-down Therapy Companion Animal of the Year thumps his tail and wriggles impishly. Joanne can't help getting up to rub his belly and Willie closes his eyes in bliss. Both rest securely, knowing the other's care and devotion is total and unqualified. Moments later, Joanne hears her big dog snoring.

For Joanne, even a sleeping, noisily reverberating Willie is comforting. He is at her side, ready to help if she needs him. She thinks of the good times, and the times that aren't so bad because Willie is there to look out for her. She wants to hug him. She begins to say, "You're a good boy, Willie," then decides to keep quiet, to let him sleep.

NOVA SCOTIA, CANADA

HONEY HURRICANE

The sun shines brightly on two-year-old Honey Hurricane as she takes her last run with Jean near the pond behind their prison housing unit. Jean has known this day would come ever since she was first given Honey to train as a service dog. Honey, a cross between a cocker spaniel and a Nova Scotia duck tolling retriever, has been her inseparable companion for almost a year. And Jean has loved her and bonded with her as she has with no other creature.

Today it is time to say good-bye.

They walk slowly to the canine room in the main building of Nova Institution, a medium-security prison in Truro, Nova Scotia. The room is filled with fluorescent-lit plants and images of women and dogs, including the participants of the Pawsitive Directions Canine Program. Jean Reynolds, a tall thirty-eight-year-old with a shock of curly brown hair, crouches down to be close to tiny, golden-brown Honey Hurricane, who stands less than knee high.

No long good-byes. Jean wraps her arms around Honey and gives her a final kiss. Honey seems subdued. She doesn't leap up on Jean or show excitement. "After all the time we spent together, she knows something is going on," Jean quickly realizes. "She's probably been picking up vibes from me all week."

Jean strides toward the door to return to her room. Normally, Honey would accompany her. But, today, when she faithfully follows, Jean turns and says, "You stay here, Honey."

Honey's round brown eyes soulfully follow Jean's retreating figure. She curls up in a tight ball on the floor, waiting out this latest change in a young life filled with turbulence and transformation.

Honey's known biography begins in the Colchester County pound. Animal control officer John Sitser found her starving and abandoned, running wild on the streets of Truro.

She was pacing in an outdoor pen with five or six other yelping dogs when Heather Logan came to adopt a dog for the prison canine program. According to pound rules, Honey would be destroyed if nobody adopted her within the next forty-eight hours.

Heather, a no-nonsense dog breeder and trainer with thirty years' experience, checked out the dogs. Her adoption guidelines were strict: no dogs with even the slightest sign of aggression; and no guard breeds such as German shepherds, who could potentially be trained to protect the prisoners against the guards.

"Are you interested in this little brown dog?" asked animal control officer John Sitser.

Based on her breeding, Honey had the credentials to fit Heather's bill. Cocker spaniels are highly intelligent, friendly, and exuberant. As an added bonus, they are often hopeless guard dogs. Jaunty, animated Nova Scotia duck tolling retrievers—tollers, for short—were developed in the nineteenth century to attract and retrieve ducks. The flash and bounce of the white points on their paws, chests, and tails seemed to lure ducks to the blind. Tollers are smart, devoted to children and families, and take well to obedience training. Like cocker spaniels, they can be wonderfully inadequate guard dogs.

"No," Heather answered inexplicably, and she left, alone.

Ten days later, Heather came back. And, surprisingly, Honey was still there. Once again, softhearted John asked Heather if she wanted the little brown dog. Once again, Heather said no.

Another ten days passed, and when Heather returned to the pound, Honey was still there. John saw something special in her and thought she'd make a really nice pet. That's why he hung on to her. This time, John insisted on knowing why Heather wouldn't take her.

Honey jumped at the wire fence, trying desperately to capture Heather's attention. Heather considered John's question and realized that her refusal was based completely on personal prejudice. "Spaniel-like dogs don't seem to get along with me," she admitted. "They've bitten me many times in the past thirty years."

In order to be fair, Heather agreed to behavior-test Honey, to see if she allowed herself to be handled and to ensure she was not aggressive.

John opened the cage, and Honey bounded out, wiggling and wagging her tail, straight into Heather's arms.

Meanwhile, at Nova Institution, inmate Jean Reynolds successfully completed phase one of the three-phase canine program, covering the theory of canine behavior and training. She then asked Heather hopefully if she could have her own dog to train, a large, black male, if possible.

When Heather returned to Nova, she called Jean to meet her out front.

Jean saw her approaching in the distance, with a little brown creature flipping around at the end of a leash like a hooked fish.

"Here's your dog," Heather said, "except she's not large, not black, and not male."

Jean looked at the dog. The dog looked up at her and it was love at first sight. Jean got down on her knees, and although Honey was filthy, she enveloped the small dog in a tight hug.

"Oh, honey," she sighed. Then she thought a moment and smiled up at Heather. "That's her name."

A few days later, with a better understanding of her new dog, Jean added the surname Hurricane. Honey Hurricane was everywhere at once, getting into it all.

Jean and Honey began training, two newcomers on a journey together. Jean's experience with animals was limited and Honey, the street survivor, growled defensively whenever other dogs approached. She launched herself ferociously at Heather's massive German shepherd. Jean was horrified, thinking that Honey was about to become lunch, but the larger, gentle pet was well-behaved.

Honey's socialization began with a down-stay command and a gradual acclimatization to being circled and stepped over by eight other dogs. As long as she stayed down, Jean praised her lavishly and handed out goodies, until

Honey understood that staying down earned her treats. Eventually, she learned to remain still for longer and longer stretches.

Next was heeling. Jean placed a strip of tape on the side of her left leg, just below the knee, as a marker. Honey had to control her exuberance and stay within six inches of the little piece of tape. Heeling calmly by her trainer didn't come naturally. "We played statue a lot," Jean recalls. Whenever her dog rushed ahead, Jean stood still until Honey caught on that she wouldn't get anywhere faster by racing ahead.

At the end of November, three months after Honey and Jean met, their relationship was abruptly terminated by Jean's parole. Thrilled to be out of prison, Jean bade Nova adieu, and wrote a heart-wrenching farewell poem to Honey.

Even when we're far apart
I'll hold your memory in my heart
The bond we share no one can break
Though when you're gone my heart will ache.
So here's my heart
It belongs to you
I love you, Honey,
You know I do.

Honey returns to the kennel at Heather's to await a new trainer. Jean heads to Halifax, violates her parole conditions by drinking, and within three weeks is returned to Nova with no guarantee of getting Honey back. And now she needs and wants her more than ever.

Then Jean gets good news. She is being given another chance in the canine program. Honey rushes up to her, tail wagging, ecstatic to see her again. After weeks of being just "a happy kennel dog," Honey's skills have regressed, but she is blessed with high intelligence and a persistent nature.

The team quickly falls into step with each other, deepening their bond and undertaking more advanced training.

Most mornings, the other three dogs sharing their house leave their trainers' rooms and galumph into Jean's room for a doggie rumpus. Then Honey and Jean take a long walk around the grounds, often with at least one other inmate-dog team. While Jean works in maintenance and horticulture, Honey returns to her crate in their room. For at least two hours every weekday, rain or shine, Honey and her mistress walk together. They also spend an hour training with Heather, practicing everything from skipping rope in tandem to retrieving a soft drink from the fridge. Weekends, Jean and Honey often spend five hours together walking, training, and enjoying each other's company.

In April, after eight months of training, Jean learns Honey is going to the Braeside Nursing Home to start her career as a nursing-home assistance dog. To further prepare her for her new job, Jean teaches Honey to lay her head quietly on her knee and wait to be petted. She plays "old lady" with a walker, making sure Honey stays clear of her uncertain movements. Using a wheelchair, she helps Honey readjust her previous heeling technique. Honey learns to let the wheelchair move through the door first before returning to a proper heel. Finally, Jean introduces a bell hanging by the door, so Honey can ring it to attract attention when she needs to go out.

At the end of the month, Honey takes her Canine Good Citizen test, administered by the American Kennel Club. She demonstrates her proficiency in the fundamentals of dog obedience, including greeting new dogs, heeling, and walking on a loose leash. Eight months earlier, Honey had instinctively attacked a large German shepherd. Now, having passed her tests with flying colors, she is officially decreed a model canine citizen.

Soon after, Jean is released from prison.

Three days later, Honey moves to her new residence, the Braeside Nursing Home in the tiny village of Middle Musquodoboit.

Some Cute Dog

Honey lies awake in her spacious metal crate in the activity-planning office at Braeside Nursing Home, on the banks of a peaceful river valley. She is partly covered with a pink blanket, her rope toy and bone beside her. It's 6:30 A.M., the time she used to awaken beside Jean, leaping all over her bed, covering her with kisses, begging to run outdoors right away.

A staff member unlatches Honey's crate and wishes her a cheery good morning. Without further ado, the new nursing-home assistance dog bounds out, eager to start the day.

Her white paws pad down the pastel-painted hallway, through the activity room, and straight to the back door. Honey makes a beeline for the fenced-in yard and, true to her retriever self, tears around enthusiastically until she's spent. She rests briefly in the shade, tracking the birds overhead until it's time for morning rounds.

Cathie Risser, the personal care worker primarily responsible for Honey, sets the room-to-room pace. Honey seems to know instinctively how to behave with those in wheelchairs and those with dementia or Alzheimer's. She approaches them slowly and moves gently near them.

Esther, who has severe dementia, speaks rarely, and when she does, it's one labored word at a time. Cathie positions Honey in front of the elderly resident and the old woman's hands immediately seek out her soft fur.

"You're some cute dog!" Esther says effortlessly.

Cathie rewards the friendly dog with a handful of dried food. Honey was trained using a method called operant conditioning. Based on the principles of psychologist B. F. Skinner, operant conditioning uses only positive reinforcement, and Honey's daily ration of dog food is meted out one treat at a time all day long. She earns her tasty reinforcement by working, embedding the notion that positive behavior leads to concrete rewards. Cathie wears a pouch with treats on her waist and a bowl of food sits on the counter near the door for other staff members to use.

The four white paws continue along to Alice Cook's private room. It's the first of Honey's thrice daily visits. Alice is already seated near the window when Cathie arrives. Her face lights up when she sees Honey. Should Cathie ever visit without her four-legged assistant, Alice's first question is, "Where's the dog?" She opens her arms and Honey leaps up on her lap and lays her head on Alice's shoulder in a gracious canine hug. Alice knows how her visitor loves to be petted, and with trembling hands she strokes her long fur, dog and human almost purring. For Alice, it was hard to leave her dairy farm and her big old house to come to Braeside nine months ago. But the hardest part was leaving behind her collie, Keesha. Widowed for twelve years, Alice had treasured Keesha's companionship. Now, when Cathie waves good-bye, she leaves a new canine friend with the resident. Honey remains, always nearby but never underfoot, keeping Alice company.

Honey visits from room to room, cheering the residents with her warm, life-affirming presence. When she's invited, she jumps up onto the bed, laying her head on a resident's lap, waiting to be petted. When she first arrived, she was so excited about her new surroundings, she couldn't sit still for a moment. Now she can lie quietly for short periods, while gentle hands stroke her head. Cathie encourages her with treats, hoping that eventually Honey will settle in for prolonged periods, offering comfort to those who are frail and bedridden.

At 8:00 A.M., Honey returns to her pink blanket for a much-needed break. While the residents eat, she rests, preparing for more morning visits. As with any nursing-home worker, there's a danger of burnout. Being constantly enthusiastic and energetic with so many people can be exhausting. Honey stretches out and enjoys the downtime.

By mid-morning, she has visited everybody who wants her company, and she's ready for another run outside. A cowbell hangs waist-high at the back door for Honey, but for some reason she doesn't like its sound. She jumps up next to it, but avoids ringing it. When a staff member goes out to grab a breath of air, she dashes out, darting left and right, scampering around the picnic table, churning up the yard with her little legs.

A decorated pineapple sits on the table in the small kitchen area; a mechanical parrot flies in circles from a center ceiling beam; and the Hawaiian luau begins. Honey dashes around the activity room, trailing a tissue-paper lei from her mouth, twisting her head back and forth, toying with the lei until it shreds. She spots the mechanical bird and her hunting-dog instinct awakens. She jumps at it with youthful abandon.

Cathie hands out Hula Hoops to two volunteers and calls Honey to participate in a little entertainment. The volunteers hold up the hoops in a row. Honey sits. Then Cathie commands, "Hoop, hoop, bell!" and Honey vaults through the hoops, heading for her target—the cowbell at the door. She leaps toward it, veers to the side in mid-jump, and bypasses the bell, nosing the doorframe instead.

"She faked me out!" Cathie whoops, remembering Honey's aversion to the sound of that bell.

Honey drifts out of the room and sees Hugh, dressed in a red shirt and blue slacks, sitting in his wheelchair. Nobody knows what's on Hugh's mind, since he rarely speaks, and when he does he is not always lucid. Honey visits him at least three times a day.

"Where's your puppy?" Cathie asks him, as she moves to the side of his wheelchair and taps his knee.

"Knee," she says to Honey.

Honey places her head on Hugh's knee and waits there patiently. Cathie reaches into her pouch to hand Hugh the doggie treat, and his eyes shine merrily as his fingers close around it. He hesitates slightly, then offers it to her, remembering from her many visits how gentle she is.

Cathie redirects Honey's attention to Martha, fidgeting nervously on the couch beside Hugh's wheelchair.

"Get out! Get out!" Martha yells, lifting her cane.

"You liked her this morning," Cathie reminds her. "You were calling her kitty-kitty!"

"I don't want a bit of it," Martha responds, but a smile creeps across her face. Cathie takes the old woman's cane-free hand and gently places it on Honey's back. Martha begins caressing Honey, slowly, rhythmically. The small brown dog snuggles in close. As she repetitively strokes the soft warm fur, Martha's blood pressure stabilizes. By the time the luau is over, she is fast asleep.

·   ·   ·

In the early evening, Honey does her final rounds, including another trip to Alice's room. Alice invites her onto the bed and takes out her dog brush. Honey flips over on her back, legs stretched in the air, waiting to be petted. Then she rights herself, tail wagging in anticipation as Alice's trembling hands lift the brush and lovingly run it down the length of the little dog's back. As Alice strokes, her shaking completely ceases and her movements become firm and calm.

At the community college in Truro, where she's studying to become a veterinary assistant, Jean still thinks of Honey and the bond they shared. "Honey needed a whole lot of love, and I had a whole lot to give her." Jean realizes that, through her dog, she experienced a unique love that gave her confidence and changed her life profoundly.

Now, Honey takes all the love Jean first gave her and shares it with a dozen elderly people. As Alice fondly untangles the feathery knots behind the little brown dog's ears, she sighs contentedly. "With Honey here, this place feels more like home." Once again, Alice has someone loving to care for.

Nightfall ends Honey's long shift. She eats a last evening snack and curls up in her cozy crate, a small castaway mutt graced with the gift of reawakening love and hope in all those her little body touches.

PART SIX

ECO DOGS

. . . .

NAMIBIA, AFRICA

FLINTIS

A soft rustle in the thornbushes beyond the pasture causes Flintis to turn his head as he walks ahead of his flock. The Anatolian shepherd stops, turns, sniffs the air... it reeks of danger, of death. He emits a low, growling snarl, then barks louder, more urgently. Humanlike creatures appear behind the sheep. A troop of baboons. Forty of them move in among the ewes and lambs, looking curiously at the fluffy white ungulates, a treacherous situation for livestock, primates, and dog.

No more warning barks. Flintis confronts the unfamiliar threat. The troop's dominant males, two fierce fighters who have battled their way to this position, refuse to back down. They have females and young to feed. But Flintis has a family to protect. Teeth bared, Flintis faces the baboons in a combat that dogs have never been known to win.

. . .

Bravery, such as that shown by Flintis, cannot be taught. It must be bred into a dog over generations. In the rural areas of Turkey, Anatolian shepherds have watched over nomads' flocks since at least 1800 B.C. As the men of these nomadic Turkish tribes roamed the plains looking for fresh pastures, the defense of livestock and family encampments was entrusted to large dogs. The best dogs were those who stayed close to camp and didn't waste time chasing animals. Dogs who protected livestock were revered; all others were expendable.

Over time, a group of large, fast-moving canines evolved. Living an isolated existence on the empty plains of central Anatolia, the breed remained relatively unchanged through succeeding generations. When Anatolian shepherds were eventually imported to the United States, they were employed to guard livestock, and word spread of their protective prowess against large predators such as wolves and cougars. But there is perhaps no place where these dogs are valued more than in the heart of Africa, where they guard against the fastest hunter on earth, the African cheetah.

These yellow, black-spotted cats ("cheetah" is the Hindi word for "spotted one") are forced to prey on livestock because of their shrinking natural habitat. Capable of sprinting up to seventy-five miles per hour, cheetahs are the scourge of ranchers in the African outback. Yet the cheetah population is also extremely fragile. Twelve thousand years ago, isolation and inbreeding began a genetic bottleneck in the cheetah population, and now all cheetahs share ninety-nine percent of the same genetic material. A disease that threatens one threatens all the cheetahs in its area. They are, according to the World Conservation Union, "critically endangered."

African ranchers have tried many methods to protect their herds, including the use of Border collies. But the collie's response to predators, an "eye-stalk-chase" sequence, inevitably caused the livestock to panic and flee. High-speed predators such as cheetahs start hunting when their prey break into a run. The collie's actions inadvertently triggered this instinct. The rancher's last resort was to kill the cheetahs, or trap and remove them.

In 1991, concerned about cheetah extinction, Laurie Marker helped establish the Cheetah Conservation Fund (CCF) on eighteen thousand acres outside Otjiwarongo, Namibia. Marker's goal is to save the largest concentration of cheetahs in Africa, the 2,500 Namibian cheetahs. When she first arrived in Namibia, she recognized the inherent drawback to using herding dogs, like collies, to guard African livestock. Having worked with Anatolian shepherds in the United States, she understood the breed's instinctive "approach-withdraw reaction" to threats. She also knew that "protection is part and parcel of their genetics." Marker had a gut feeling that she had found the perfect African guard dog and a solution to the rancher's conflict with cheetahs. "By doing such a complete job of protecting livestock," she reasoned, "Anatolian shepherds have shown that they can save and protect cheetahs, too."

Death in the Air

The sheep are asleep in the corral and Flintis lies outside the gate. In the cool hours of the first light, predators stalk the tempting ewes and lambs, the corral fences providing no deterrent. Death lurks in the deceptive calm before dawn.

Flintis's wake-up call is a twig snapped by a jackal prowling among the low bushes surrounding the enclosure. Flintis springs to his feet, moves toward the sound, and barks once, low and aggressively. The jackal flees. Flintis returns to his post and lies back down.

Two, four, five times, jackals push close to the corral and each time Flintis guards his flock. Warn, wait until the threat is gone, return to post. In the early morning hours, jackal, hyena, caracal, and civet all visit the livestock corral. Flintis frightens them away, never giving chase. Hunting the intruder

would be the natural reaction of most canines, but Flintis's ancestors are of a different bloodline, bred not to attack but to protect.

Now the sun is hot, the air filled with the pungent aroma of acacia bushes in bloom. The corral gates swing open. Flintis stands erect, tail wagging, as his sheep wander out and surround him. He sniffs each one.

"Come, Flintis," his owner, rancher Johann Coetzee, calls.

Flintis approaches Johann, accepting a few pats on the head, and lets his friend ruffle his fur, checking for ticks. But when the rancher turns to wave at Bernard, his herdsman, Flintis quickly grabs the opportunity to rejoin the sheep.

Tail pointed, head high, Flintis leads them to pasture. Flintis's short, coarse coat, highly adapted to the freezing winters and dry, hot summers of central Anatolia, is perfectly suited to the climate of the Namibian outback. In Afrikaans, "flintis" means rag, or, more accurately, "shmatte," the Yiddish word for an old, almost worthless piece of clothing. It's what Johann thought Flintis would look like after spending weeks outside in the hot, dusty weather.

Unfazed by the searing heat, Flintis relaxes under the shade of a baobab tree. The mere presence of this broad-shouldered, 140-pound dog is usually enough to keep predators away. But today, a hungry cheetah, chased off a kill by scavenging hyenas, creeps quietly through the tall, brown grass at pasture's edge. Padded feet dampen the sounds of its footsteps, but to Flintis's keen ears, the cheetah's steps echo like drumbeats. Flintis leaps up and advances toward the sound. The older sheep slowly move in the direction the dog's tail is pointing, behind their "big brother," to safety. The younger animals follow. There is no panic. One stern bark and the big cat is gone.

The herdsman observes Flintis's work from a small rise, but does not interfere. Anatolian shepherds work best alone. All through Flintis's training, human contact was discouraged. From the age of six weeks, Flintis lived, ate, and slept with Johann's livestock. In the mornings, he took short treks with the herd and spent the rest of the day with the lambs. Since the livestock were his only true companions, Flintis began to bond with the sheep. But when Flintis was nine weeks old, the herdsman reported a problem to Johann. The puppy was chasing small lambs, an unpardonable sin for a guard dog. Flintis would have to be shipped back to the Cheetah Conservation Fund. Johann resigned himself to more livestock losses and, worse, to killing more cheetahs. Yet something about the gregarious pup prompted Johann to observe him for one more day. What he saw made him smile.

Flintis and the lambs were lying together in the shade. As some lambs rose and drifted into the sun, Flintis instinctively redirected them back to the shade. Like generations of Anatolian shepherds before him, Flintis had imprinted on the sheep. He thought he was one of them. They were, for all intents and purposes, his family.

. . .

Before Flintis came to the farm, Johann had suffered huge livestock losses. Predators killed forty-two sheep in one night and another twenty-nine one evening soon after. Johann used to kill cheetahs to protect his livelihood. But since Flintis's arrival six years ago, cheetahs don't stay around long enough to be a nuisance. Working tirelessly through hot African days and dark, perilous nights, Flintis protects both livestock and cheetahs.

"That's a dog who loves his work," Johann thinks, allowing himself a softness for his black-masked, fawn-colored dog, whom even a hardened Namibian rancher can't resist.

Another slight noise, this time a jackal. Most of Johann's losses occur at night, when the flock is in the corral, but today there is activity on the plains. Flintis is up and moves toward the intruder.

This time, no bark is required; the jackal retreats. Flintis is so good at the classic "approach-withdraw" behavior that since he began working, Johann has not lost any livestock. Nor has he had to remove any cheetahs from his land.

Five, six times that day, Flintis warns off threats to the herd.

In the late afternoon, the herdsman drives the large flock toward home. Flintis is in front, with the flock strung out three hundred yards behind him.

From his porch, out of the heat of the setting sun, Johann sees the tall, rangy herdsman pushing his three hundred sheep toward the corral, the Saint Bernard–sized Flintis in the lead. Johann regards his dog appreciatively. The sheep represent the major part of Johann's farm income, and Flintis is the family's insurance policy against livestock loss.

Then, suddenly, the fifty-two-year-old rancher hears Flintis bark out a warning.

"Stop or I will stop you," it seems that Flintis is warning the intruder.

"Hurry," the bark says to Johann.

By the time Johann reaches the sheep, the herdsman has joined up with him. Perhaps by chance, perhaps to kill, a troop of baboons has infiltrated the flock. The men hear terrifying noises in the bush. Together they rush toward the screams of the baboons and Flintis's furious growls.

Then, ominously, the plains fall silent.

The herdsman and Johann stop. They scan the terrain, searching over and around the thornbushes for a glimpse of Flintis.

A baboon screech signals a renewed attack. Incredibly, the fight is still on. The two men run toward the awful sounds and make a gruesome discovery. There, on the ground by a large rock, is a dead baboon, its neck torn open. In the distance, they hear Flintis locked in vicious, mortal combat with the second baboon.

Away from Johann and the herdsman, Flintis fights unprepared and alone. He is trained to scare off predators or, at worst, clamp down his jaws in a controlled bite until his master arrives. But this battle is beyond holding and waiting. It is, inexorably, a fight to the death.

Crashing through the underbrush for more than a mile, Flintis battles the second baboon. Something deep inside the Anatolian shepherd drives him on. Nothing in his past training or ancestry has prepared him for these bizarre creatures that just won't quit.

Dog and baboon come together one last time, the baboon lashing out with his forepaws and slashing Flintis with his teeth. Flintis weakens with loss of blood, but at the very last moment, perhaps driven by what might happen to the herd if he should fail, he twists his head and grabs the baboon by the neck.

When Johann and the herdsman arrive, the baboon and Flintis lie silent on the ground. The baboon is dead and they are sure Flintis is, too. His body is covered in blood; his back torn open, revealing his backbone. Sadness wrinkling his eyes, Johann bends down close to his guard dog, his friend. What he sees shocks him. Flintis is alive. Barely breathing, but alive.

They carry Flintis back to a shady spot at the corral, where Johann administers daily doses of penicillin. For five days, the fallen dog takes neither food nor water. On the sixth day, Flintis drinks from his water bowl and eats a few mouthfuls. Eight days after the baboon attack, he staggers to his feet to rejoin the herd, and has to be restrained. Later, he chews through his rope and limps over to his sheep, only to collapse among them. He has to be chained, until he finally regains his strength and returns to guard his flock.

. . .

Johann is amazed that Flintis survived the attack. The CCF had already lost one guard dog to baboons and the staff can hardly believe that two baboons are dead. Widely reported throughout Namibia, Flintis's feat encourages ranchers to inquire about the guard dog program. Because of Flintis, more cheetahs will be saved. But heroic Flintis, oblivious to all the attention, tends to his sheep. Anxiously he sniffs each member of his flock, not satisfied until he has accounted for every one.

Although Flintis abhors leaving his flock, the CCF requests his services shortly after his recovery. Johann escorts him to the Otjiwarongo breeding farm to meet Boots, a female Anatolian shepherd. Thirteen squiggly puppies are born from this happy union, and now most guard Namibian flocks. These puppies in turn will have their own progeny, increasing the pool of seventy-five Anatolian shepherds now active in the African outback.

At seven years of age, Flintis continues to protect Johann's sheep, and his powerful instinct to risk his life for his flock now courses through the bloodlines of fearless guard dogs throughout Namibia.

. . . .

CRICKET

O I OO hours, Andersen Air Force Base, Guam, South Pacific.

Despite the hour, Jeeps and trucks dart like ants from airplane to airplane; soldiers fuel, load, and repair; planes taxi and take off; a transport tugs a landed C-5 into its bay.

Across the black asphalt, four tiny white paws pad through the tide of human and mechanical traffic.

Cricket, a seven-year-old black, white, and tan Jack Russell terrier, stops and waits patiently as his handler, Anthony Manibusan, runs a finger carefully down the Air Traffic Operations manifest on his clipboard. Cricket looks up as an Air Command jet roars off the runway and arcs gracefully into the sky.

Anthony nods toward a Hawaii-bound C-141 parked in the nearest airplane slot. Cricket tugs lightly, leaning forward on his leash. Body tense, steps quick and deliberate, he leads Anthony toward the enormous cargo plane. The plane is stuffed with harmless peacetime cargo—extra helmets for training in Okinawa, kitchen supplies for an army base in Saipan, extra beds for a barracks in Hawaii.

But the plane itself is a battleground in a difficult environmental war, one in which the twelve-inch-high, seventeen-pound canine is a specially trained soldier on full alert. His enemy is the brown tree snake, an insidious serpent that threatens life and property. Cricket's mission is simple: find the four- to ten-foot-long venomous snakes before they escape from Guam to wreak ecological havoc elsewhere.

In its native Australasian ecosystem, the brown tree snake, *Boiga irregularis,* is easily controlled by its natural avian and mammalian predators. But fifty years ago, a few of these large arboreal reptiles, probably from Papua New Guinea, stowed away on a ship to Guam. They thrived in this hot, humid, predator-free climate, devouring birds, lizards, and eggs of wild and domestic fowl. By the 1970s, when officials finally realized that the snake had to be controlled, more than a million reptiles, up to thirteen thousand snakes per square mile, had slithered through the waist-high grass and tangled brush into every nook and cranny of Guam. The ko ko', an indigenous flightless bird, was wiped out, the Marianas fruit bat and the Guam gecko hover close to extinction, and twelve species of native birds, some found nowhere else, have disappeared from the island. The brown tree snake climbs wooden power poles, crawls along the vine-like electrical wires, and hides in transformers, shorting them out and causing an average of one electrical outage every three days since 1989. In their own struggle to survive, the snakes push into cities and have bitten over two hundred people, seventy-four of them toddlers, most attacked as they slept.

Although the people of Guam seem to have adjusted to the snake, Hawaii, a major flight destination three thousand miles west and home to forty-one percent of America's endangered birds, waits and worries. Even one Hawaiian power outage can cost millions of dollars on that glittering tourist playground. Seven snakes have already been found crawling out of airplane landing gear in Hawaii. "Keep the snakes in Guam" was the lobbying cry of Hawaiian representatives in Washington. The result: 2.6 million dollars was appropriated by Congress to fight the snakes.

Enter Cricket, one of the thirteen Jack Russell terriers stationed on Guam since 1993.

The instinct that drives Cricket to fearlessly seek out a poisonous animal much larger than himself lies deep in his bloodline. In the mid-1800s, Reverend John (nicknamed Jack) Russell, a British parson and sportsman, began breeding a dog that went to ground quickly, following its prey so tenaciously it would dig into burrows and tunnels, often completely disappearing from sight until it cornered and killed its prey. Thus it was given the name terrier, from the Latin word *terra,* meaning earth. Russell crossbred the best working terriers he could find, including fox, Scottish, and Welsh terriers. The result was a wire-haired, compact, flexible dog, somewhat resembling its quarry— groundhogs, badgers, and foxes. For much of the twentieth century, Jack Russell terriers were renowned hunters and remain physiologically stable except for an uncontrollable variation in color, which prevents their acceptance as an official American Kennel Club breed. Jack Russell terriers represent a canine husbandry based on talent, intelligence, and courage rather than looks. They continue to thrive under an unknown number of breed standards, and remain an admired, if unofficial, breed.

The Watch That Never Ends

Cricket lies on his padded sleeping platform, unfazed by the deep-throated German shepherd barks reverberating off the concrete kennel walls. He and

his fellow snake dogs share the military working dog (MWD) barracks with six big, tough attack dogs, bomb sniffers, and drug dogs. The continuing ruckus tells Cricket someone has entered the compound. He hops down and goes to the kennel gate. It's midnight and he knows his graveyard shift is about to begin. When the gate opens, Cricket is ready, his stubby tail wagging a frenetic greeting to his partner, Anthony, wildlife services agent, U.S. Department of Agriculture (USDA).

The small brown-eared terrier trots out into the warm, moonless February night. He stretches his legs in the exercise yard, keeping a close eye on Anthony, and when his handler opens the back door of a dark, government-issue Chevy Blazer, Cricket races over and leaps three times his height up into his travel cage. He sits alertly in the back while Anthony drives around the air base perimeter, the powerful rooftop searchlight illuminating the ground along a high chain-link fence. A long, dark form slithers under the bright light. The Blazer stops and Anthony jumps out. He snatches the snake deftly with snake tongs, puts it in a burlap bag, and, in deference to Cricket, ties it to the side mirror of the truck. "If I put it in the truck, the smell would drive

Cricket crazy." Even so, Cricket stands excitedly, tail wagging. He can almost taste snake.

Anthony stops at one of the airplane hangars and checks in with the USDA wildlife services office. The night controller's update lists three outbound flights en route to "high priority" target areas—islands with hot, humid climates and plenty of easy prey, ideal for the *Boiga irregularis* snake to survive and multiply.

> 0230: C-130 to Hickam Air Force Base in Hawaii
> 0500: C-5 to Okinawa
> 0645: civilian flight to Honolulu

At 0200, Cricket's Blazer pulls onto the tarmac of the main runway of the 634th squadron, dwarfed by the C-130 military transport. Two crewmen, just completing the final checklist, stand down as Cricket hops out of the Blazer. Orders from the Pentagon carry a lot of weight, and Hawaii's powerful congressman has made it clear that everyone is to cooperate with the snake patrol. Cricket lifts his head so Anthony can attach his leash and the team approaches the six-foot-high tires under the belly of the plane. It seems impossible that any animal could climb those tires, but tree snakes can hold their bodies erect for almost their entire four- to ten-foot length. *B. irregularis* hunts by night, and in daylight it seeks out a dark hiding spot. After a night of hunting lizards on the airport runway, it finds a convenient rubber tire to climb and works its way into the landing gear of waiting planes. There, they are almost impossible to detect.

"Find it," Anthony whispers, and Cricket sniffs the ground around each wheel, showing little interest.

"Atta boy, good boy," Anthony encourages.

At the last tire, Cricket wags his tail, and Anthony lifts him up to investigate further, into the wheel housing. The dog disappears and emerges a brief second later, convincing Anthony that this C-130 to Hawaii is clean. Anthony signals the crew that the search is complete.

"Up you go," he calls to a clearly downcast Cricket, and gently shuts the Blazer's door.

The next flight leaves at 0500, and it's still too early to check the plane. The inspection must be close enough to departure time so that snakes can't slither up into the landing gear after Anthony and Cricket have finished. The team takes advantage of the preflight lag time to plug another port of exit—the 634th squadron freight yard.

Cricket's tail thumps the side of his transport cage. He knows that cargo patrol offers the best chance of finding a snake—crawling up a pallet, slinking through the netting, on the move.

Cricket walks on a short, tight rein, then suddenly tugs on the leash. Anthony shines his beam in the direction Cricket is pulling. "Nighttime is cane toad time, as poisonous as nerve gas," Anthony thinks. He squints into the gloom, shaking his head at how badly human commerce has unbalanced the Guam ecosystem. An Australian native snake is passing through Guam to get to Hawaii, while Hawaii exports the deadly poisonous cane toad to Guam. The poison of the dull brown frog could be lethal for an instinctive hunter like Cricket.

"Whoa." Anthony pulls back on the leash gently, patting Cricket. But Cricket's nose stays on the ground sniffing, his tail erect. "It's more than a cane toad," Anthony knows instantly. Jack Russells generally hunt by sight, but for this job, Cricket has been trained to track by scent. When he sniffs, it means snake.

"Where is it?" Anthony asks. Cricket strains against the leash, pulling Anthony between two rows of crates, HAWAII stenciled on their sides. At a covered drain, the little terrier runs back and forth, tugging on the leash, keening in a constant, high-pitched whimper.

"Sit," Anthony orders, reining Cricket in. Cricket sits, every muscle in his body quivering and taut. His rump moves back and forth across the ground, his front paws step in place.

Anthony bends and lifts the sheet of metal on the ground.

A large-headed, bulging-eyed, seven-foot snake slithers toward the containers.

Silently, Anthony unhooks the leash. Cricket needs no spoken order. Hair bristling, ears forward, jaw muscles clenched, Cricket launches himself. Anthony holds his breath. The snake has no time to turn and coil or strike. With a tenacity that surprises even his experienced handler, Cricket grabs the snake behind the neck, lifts the six-pound reptile clear off the ground, and shakes it ferociously, killing it. It takes no more than three seconds. Then he lets it drop to the ground and returns to Anthony's side.

Anthony exhales, relieved.

"So much fury in such a small package," he thinks.

He places the snake in a burlap burial bag, strokes Cricket's head, and thoroughly checks his paws and flanks for wounds. There is a small, superficial fang mark on Cricket's front leg. Cleaning the wound with an antiseptic kept ready in the glove compartment, Anthony considers the qualities that make Cricket perfect for one thing and dreadfully unsuited to another.

Cricket's former owners, an elderly California couple, couldn't handle his high energy and love of exercise. The answer to their dilemma was a USDA advertisement offering homes for unwanted Jack Russell terriers. Two-year-old Cricket's next stop was Guam. There, he faced a pass-or-fail USDA "temperament" test. The trainer threw a large brown tree snake onto the ground in the exercise yard in front of Cricket. If Cricket ran away or showed fear, his career as a snake hunter was over. "We can't train them if they don't have the basic game instinct," Anthony knows from experience. But Cricket was on to the snake so quickly that the trainer saw instantly he was a natural, proving Anthony's dictum that "there is nothing more powerful than a blood drive." The energy and stamina that made Cricket such a demanding pet also made him an ideal recruit for the snake program.

Cricket was chosen to undergo prey-kill training. Live brown tree snakes, like the one Anthony bagged at the fence, were rubbed along the ground to leave a scent trail, then hidden from sight in the grass. At the key words "find it," Cricket learned to sniff the trail and track the scent, his reward the snake itself.

"Now no one questions Cricket's snake-finding abilities," says his proud handler.

0400: an hour before the C-5 flight departs for Okinawa.

Despite the late hour, the earlier find and kill has left Cricket energized and craving more action. When Anthony opens the Blazer door, Cricket flies into his car cage. Back through the chain-link fence, onto the tarmac, and out

to the giant C-5 plane. Carefully, Cricket sniffs the wheels, lifts one paw, and looks up. "Hmmm, perhaps a snake in the housing," Anthony thinks. "Only one way to find out." Anthony lifts Cricket up into the gear housing. Cricket disappears in one side and scrambles quickly out the other.

Second high-priority plane, all clear.

0545: The rising sun paints the ocean a fiery orange as Cricket inspects a commercial 747 jet destined to be filled with islanders on a shopping junket to Honolulu. Once again, the feisty terrier's thorough reconnaissance certifies the airliner snake free.

Last high-priority plane, all clear.

0800. Anthony stops at the USDA office to telephone the night controller. Orders are to stay available until his shift ends at nine, just in case there are any unscheduled flights.

0900. Back at the kennel, the shift finally over, Cricket is not yet ready to call it a night. He pushes Anthony's hand with his head, then looks up beseechingly.

"Oh, okay," Anthony says, pulling a squeaky plastic hamburger from a locker. He throws it as far as he can. "Go get it."

Cricket's short little legs and heavyset body power after the toy. He pounces on it in a flash, chews it, throws it into the air, grabs it before it hits the ground, and whips it furiously from side to side.

Then he races back across the exercise field to Anthony's feet to deposit the toy. Skipping sideways, he waits for it to be thrown again, his front legs splayed like a short-limbed Bambi slipping on ice, hind legs wriggling to push his round belly across the ground.

Laughing, Anthony calls Cricket to the dog compound, and the tired terrier trots reluctantly into his kennel. He hops onto his sleeping pad and looks wistfully at the daytime-shift Jack Russell terrier heading out. Anthony smiles, knowing his dog's small body is weary but his courageous spirit is willing to battle marauding reptiles twenty-four hours a day. Tomorrow, he'll take him to the beach for a day of sun and surf, mindful that every worker needs a little rest and recreation.

Meanwhile, half an ocean away, the precious wildlife of a nation sleeps safely, thanks to the watch that never ends.

· ▪ · ▪ · ▪ · ▪ · ▪ · ▪ ·

CAPE TOWN, SOUTH AFRICA

TAMMY

Salt-laced winds blow Atlantic Ocean spray into Tammy's damp black nostrils as she sits still and focuses on the upper deck of the fisheries-inspection vessel. Oblivious to the danger ahead, she watches with one amber eye and her other blue one as her team closes in on its quarry. The lieutenant nods to his seven khaki-clad officers. Grappling hooks fly through the air and thud onto the deck of the rust-streaked trawler. Fisheries officers and police swarm onto the suspicious vessel.

Sergeant John Hennop gives a final tug on the lowering rope to make sure it's securely fastened to Tammy's boarding belt, fitted over her working harness.

"Stay, girl," he says softly, giving her a final pat.

Tammy tracks his movements as he clambers overboard, down the web ladder, and onto the boat below. In a few minutes, it will be her turn, and she sits tensely, impatient at being left behind.

The hard-faced seamen smirk as the enforcement officers shepherd them to a corner of the trawler. Having spotted the patrol, they made sure to camouflage their illegal cargo in a hold of fresh-caught snapper. They know the South African law—if no evidence is found, no charges can be filed. But the lieutenant smiles back broadly. In addition to guns, tear gas, and stun guns to protect against armed resistance, his team carries a surprise anti-poaching weapon.

Sergeant Hennop gestures to the spotlight shining down from the police boat. A form briefly obscures the light and then, out of the glare, emerge four paws, a head, black ears, and, finally, a shaggy tail. John gathers the furry bundle in his arms, lowers the small black-and-white dog onto the trawler's slippery deck, and releases the rope. Cape Town's new marine patrol dog is reporting for duty—Tammy to her friends, agent A1142 to police officials. The moment the little Border collie is aboard, the lieutenant orders the crew to open the hatches to the hold.

Tammy is the only dog in the world who can distinguish between the scent of abalone and any other type of fish. Ever since overfishing put abalone on the endangered species list, her unusual talent has become crucial to the South African Endangered Species Unit's sea operations.

Abalone thrives along shallow coasts, where the water is crystal clear. The slow-moving mollusk attaches itself to the rocks with its fleshy, mushroom-shaped foot and uses its eyes and antennae to locate marine algae, its principal food. By filtering algae from the water, these filter feeders keep the coastal aquatic ecosystem clean for other sea creatures. Abalone grows and reproduces slowly, but for the past quarter of a century, its population has augmented the meager earnings of local fishing families. Harvested properly, abalone would continue to supply food and income as well as perform its important ecological role.

Unfortunately, abalone's thick, succulent, ten-inch-long foot is much sought after in China and other Asian countries as a gourmet delicacy and as a traditional aphrodisiac. When abalone sources in North America and Australia dried up, dealers turned to South Africa, where black-market wildlife smugglers already had an established trade. Strict regulations limit the yearly abalone harvest to five hundred tons. But abalone-rich waters are also popular snorkeling areas. Since there is no law against recreational diving, poachers can easily collect their illegal catch. Also, since no law prohibits the export of other seafood from South Africa, smugglers can hide abalone in routine shipments. Under the guise of legitimate seafood exporters, the Chinese Triads, a criminal organization, control a lucrative seventeen-thousand-ton illegal abalone trade. At this rate, experts warn that abalone will be completely extinct in South Africa in less than twenty years.

For the past thirty years, dog trainers at the South African Police Dog School in Pretoria have been working with specially selected dogs to detect all manner of contraband, from explosives to rhinoceros horns and elephant tusks. "But no one ever thought it would be possible to train a dog to detect abalone," thirty-five-year-old John Hennop remembers. Tammy came to the canine academy from a family that found her too active to keep in its small yard. Like all Border collies arriving at the academy, she was first tested in sheepherding. But she showed absolutely no interest in sheep. It appeared that she would have to be put up for adoption or placed in a pound. But John, who was a trainer at the school when Tammy arrived, noticed that the homeless dog wasn't ignoring the sheep due to laziness. On the contrary, she was focusing on other objects, such as tennis balls, Frisbees, or sticks. The first time he petted her, he sensed she was somehow different from all the other dogs he'd trained. "She wouldn't take her eye off the ball. In all my fourteen years as a handler, I have never seen such intense concentration in a dog." Tammy had a highly developed sense of play, and John considered how best to harness it.

He finally made the novel and seemingly bizarre recommendation that Tammy be enlisted to help conserve the rapidly disappearing abalone.

Based on John's evaluation, Tammy was saved from the sad fate that awaited her at the city pound. Instead, the academy embarked on a secret program to determine if a dog could be trained to locate endangered shellfish. John was excused from his regular training duties to develop the world's first marine protection dog.

Eco-Agent A1142

Back on the trawler, the surly crew members resentfully open the hatches to the holds, dropping them with a loud bang.

"No abalone on this ship," the captain insists.

John leads Tammy into the middle of the tense standoff.

"Find it," he whispers.

Tammy trots across the deck, slowing to sniff at a pile of netting. She smells around the first hatch and circles a crate, nose to the deck, following an invisible trail. Suddenly, beside the second hatch, she lies down.

One of the crew members laughs, thinking the police's "secret" weapon has lost her sea legs. But John doesn't laugh. Other search dogs bark or scratch to alert their trainer, but Pretoria Academy dogs may uncover explosives or drugs coated in poison, and lying down is their prudent alert. He points his powerful flashlight into the second hold. Quickly, a police officer lowers a bucket, scoops a pile of fish, and dumps it on deck. Well hidden among the dogfish and snapper are the white shells and succulent yellow meat of abalone.

Trained to focus on the reward and not the actual find, Tammy keeps her eyes fastened on John's hands. Despite the rocking boat, the strangers, and the sound of fish slapping on the deck, only one thing interests her—the ten-

nis ball in John's right pocket. With his legs braced on the rolling deck, her trainer waves the ball in front of her nose. Tammy wraps her paws around his hand, whimpering with pleasure. He throws the ball and she catches it easily in midair. As she lands, a crew member being taken into custody stops still, staring intently, as if memorizing all Tammy's distinguishing marks and salient features. John catches the overlong examination and, sharp as lightning, feels a stab of alarm.

Two weeks earlier, during a routine airport inspection, Tammy uncovered a smuggled abalone shipment worth millions of rand. Shortly afterward, John's cell phone rang unexpectedly.

"We're going to get your dog," a low, terse voice hissed. "We know where it hides."

He heard a click, the dial tone, and the echo of someone who wanted his dog dead.

That threatening phone call was the first of many. To protect Tammy, John took her out of the police kennels and moved her to a different home every night. But even with these evening safe houses, Tammy's daily security remained a problem.

The solution proved simple and effective: Tammy got a bodyguard. Tammy was relaxing in her police kennel when she first saw her new protector, a big, lumbering German shepherd. Mac was a police attack dog with years of duty in drug busts. He had a stern air of confidence but also a playful side. Tammy carefully sniffed Mac, and the shepherd seemed to pass her silent canine personality test. Mac lowered his big head and Tammy lifted her paw to take a friendly swipe. In minutes, Tammy and her protector were racing around the kennel play area, instant bosom buddies.

With the poachers locked securely in the police van, the marine protection unit returns to police headquarters. Tammy and Mac wait expectantly in their kennels once they reach the station. They seem to sense they are still on duty and the ringing phone interrupting John's desk work proves them right. A local patrolman has spotted poachers off a beach twenty miles from Cape Town. He's calling to request the help of the canine unit.

Tammy stands by her kennel door, head raised, eager for her harness. Mac needs a bit more encouragement, but eventually bounds out of his kennel to take his place beside Tammy. With Mac and Tammy securely in their transport cages, John races through the streets of Cape Town and along the winding coastal roads. Before turning onto the narrow dirt track at False Bay, he calls for backup, then drives to a cliff overlooking the sea. The waiting patrolman points down at four men in wet suits bobbing in the surf. The two officers watch as the divers swim to shore, transporting large bags on their

backs. John waits until they finish peeling off their neoprene suits. He would feel more comfortable with backup, but he can't let the poachers escape.

As soon as John releases the latch, Tammy springs out of her cage and waits impatiently for Mac to join her. The doggie odd couple lead John down to the poachers, who have changed into street clothes and are smoking cigarettes.

"Fishing today?" John asks blandly.

"No, just swimming," one of the poachers answers.

John shrugs. He's sure he recognizes this group from a previous investigation, but without evidence, he can't arrest them.

"Go," he says sharply to Mac, letting him off his leash.

Mac trundles confidently down the beach, left, right, jogging back past John and Tammy, sniffing the boulders along the shore, checking for traps, poison, or hidden poachers. Assured the coast is clear, he returns and resumes his position beside John. Tammy gives Mac a thorough once-over, sniffing him from head to tail as if making sure her pal is okay. Only then does John undo Tammy's leash.

"Find it," he tells her.

Tammy needs no further urging. She darts along the beach, her footprints mingling with Mac's. She doubles back, then stops, nose to ground, and lifts her head, searching the breeze for a clear olfactory signal. John follows slowly, with Mac straining on his leash. Tammy hops agilely along the bleached boulders on the shore, her slim, flexible body disappearing into the cracks and crevices formed by the rocks. John struggles through the jumble and hauls himself over a large rock. At its base, he sees Tammy. She is lying at the mouth of a small cave, a flash of white plastic barely visible in the darkness within. Tammy has found the hidden abalone.

"Here's your ball," John says appreciatively, descending with Tammy's favorite toy.

John is convinced that Tammy's amazing abalone detection abilities will pave the way for teams of future "ecodogs" to protect South Africa's rich, exotic biodiversity. In 1996, after months of training in finding hidden fresh, frozen, and rotten abalone in plastic pipes, his little dog became the world's first canine to be accredited for endangered mollusk protection. "She was able to pick out the abalone even among other fish, such as snapper and tuna." With forty-five successful finds and no misses in her accreditation test, Tammy impressed even the previously skeptical police officials. "She proved herself," John asserts. "I have the utmost respect for what she can do." Soon after her final test, Tammy officially became police agent A1142 and was permanently assigned to John. For maximum efficacy, the marine protection team was transferred to South Africa's most active poaching area, the coast near Cape Town.

John pockets Tammy's toy and pulls the brimming plastic abalone pails from their rocky hiding place. Fisheries officers arrive and the poachers start to sidle down the beach, looking back nervously. An officer orders them to stop, and their leader breaks into a run. Quickly, John unhooks Mac's leash.

"Get him," he cries.

Mac sprints after the fleeing poacher and tackles him by the foot. Tammy strains on her leash, as if wanting to help, but apprehending lawbreakers is Mac's job. The big shepherd stands growling over the poacher until he is safely in handcuffs. Soon, all the poachers are rounded up and loaded into the paddy wagon.

A light rain falls as John steers home through the Cape Town rush-hour traffic. He looks back at Tammy, resting contentedly, seemingly unaffected by the race against time to preserve South African abalone. Still, it seems only fair to lighten her load, and maybe it's time for some backup. When the smuggling

dies down in the spring, John vows, he'll look for a partner to join Tammy and Mac.

John's son, Leroux, greets them excitedly at the door. "Dad, they're talking about Tammy on television." John looks at his wife, who nods affirmatively. A news reporter monitoring the police radio has noted Tammy's many successful finds and is interviewing a leader of one of the poaching syndicates. John knows him well. He is reputed to work closely with the Chinese Triads in arranging huge shipments of abalone, often in plain view of police surveillance. Abalone packed in exports of legal fish had previously frustrated any attempt to stop the illegal commerce. But Tammy has changed all that.

"Have the police been successful in curtailing the trade?" the reporter asks. The poacher laughs heartily.

"The abalone trade is too big, it is like an elephant," he says, holding his arms open wide. "I don't think the police can touch us." Then he suddenly stops laughing. "But this new dog they have, when it locates our abalone, it bites like a mosquito. And the elephant can feel it."

John picks up Leroux, who has been playing Lego fetch with Tammy, using pieces she unearthed under his bed. He hugs his small son, then lets Tammy and Mac outside. From their porch, John and Leroux gaze across the sunburned scrub and sand of the cape plains. The dogs make a strange duo, John thinks, watching them run side by side. The big shepherd and the small Border collie have no way of knowing that the Chinese Triads are part of the biggest crime organization in the world, or that their canine "ecoteam" has become the unlikely protector of a tasty, tempting filter feeder and the teeming marine waters it inhabits. They just know their jobs and do them well.

Tammy plunks a Frisbee at John's feet. Good-naturedly, he throws it across the yard. Tammy streaks after it, with Mac galloping faithfully behind.

Photo Credits

The authors would like to thank the following sources for their kind permission to reprint the photographs in this book:

Introduction
Bettmann/CORBIS, page xv
Tanya Valair, page xviii
Layne Kennedy/CORBIS,
    page xx
John Sanders, page xxi

Mas
Ferruccio Pilenga

Yanka and King
Phil Paterson, page 14
Ali Kazimi, pages 17, 18
Stephene Poulin, page 23

Star
I. G. McWilliam

AJ and Rachel
Don Harris/ UCSC Photogra-
    phy Services, pages 36, 42,
    44
Ali Kazimi, page 40

Petro
Johnston Photography

Snooper
Alfred Gordon

Bruno
Ali Kazimi, pages 66, 70, 75
Jeffrey A. Rodick, page 77

Sweep
Geoff Palfreeman

Buster
Sean Payne

Wolf
Superdogs International, page
    106
S. K. O'Neill, page 111

Happy Ralph
Marvin Gasoi, pages 116, 123,
    125
Bettmann/CORBIS, page 119

Mel
Nancy Anstruther/Freeze
    Frame, page 126
Pepita Ferrari, page 129
Alex Smith, page 134

Kavick
Mark Dumas

Elmer
©1999 Jeff Schultz/Alaska-
    Stock.com

Endal
D. M. and S. M. Parton, pages
    166, 173, 174, 179
Frank E. Naylor, page 170

Cayenne
Rosie Suissa

Willie
Joanne Weber, page 192
Flint Journal Photos/ Jane
    Hale, pages 194, 197
Doris Herber, page 200

Honey Hurricane
Stephen Moore

Flintis
Cherie Pittillo, pages 216,
    224, 225
Laurie Marker, pages 220, 222

Cricket
Dan Vice/ US Department of
    Agriculture, Wildlife Services

Tammy
Ellen Elmendorp, pages
    236 (large), 241, 246
John Stewart, pages
    236 (small), 243

Acknowledgments

This book involved a great deal of research on the life and work of dogs in many lands. Wonderful people helped us explore diverse and fascinating canine worlds, and it is our great pleasure to thank those who helped us tell these stories.

Elizabeth Klinck searched the archives, arranged photo shoots around the world, produced and cleared great visuals for every story, on deadline, and astonished us with her resourcefulness and ingenuity.

Biologist, editor, writer Martin Silverstone sussed our wavelength, hit the high notes, and never let us down.

Journalist, author Peter MacFarlane lent his fulsome talents to the task and hardly ever grumbled.

Travel journalist Cleo Paskal gave us the map we needed to organize the expedition.

Sylvain Desjardins kept the home fires warm and burning.

The fine mind and encouragement of filmmaker Anna Paskal buoyed our spirits.

And Arnie Gelbart's love, counsel, and unfailing support kept us strong.

Angela Kaye, Phil Moscovitch, Pepita Ferrari, Ana Isacson, Richard Kidder, Tom Carpenter, and David Sherman all contributed to creating layered and engaging narratives.

Our excellent literary agent, Jan Whitford, entered doggieland on a successful run, with nary a whimper.

Canadian publisher Kim McArthur, a country vet's granddaughter, infused us with her boundless energy.

The enthusiasm of our editor, Jason Kaufman at Pocket Books, and his cheerful spot-on editorial acumen, aided by his assistant, Ben Kaplan, made the publishing process a total pleasure. To Jason, for his wry, intelligent support, we owe a special debt.

Additional thanks to our coach and patriarch Sydney Weisbord, materfamilias Phyllis Amber, running partner and feeblefop storyteller par excellence Uncle H, Margo Zysman who clears the cobwebs and illuminates possibility, financial advisor Tony (Elvis) del Gaudio, our gently fierce attorney Willa Marcus, Dr. Paul Desrosiers for his inspiring professionalism, humor, and wise counsel, the personnel of the St. Therese and Lachine Veterinary Hospitals for their patience and encouragement, the fine cameraman-director Ali Kazimi, all the talented photographers who worked on this project, researcher Arlene Moscovitch, Sophie Hull for her sweet cheer, Jennifer Vaux and Melissa Maione of Galafilm, Kendra Toby, Dany Mansuy, Robert Deleskie, Bill Nemtin, herbal wizard Jackie Hazzard, Carol Lazare, Ann Charney, the "Mountain girls" from the Back Lake, all those amazing dog owners and handlers who were so generous with their time and spirit, and to our heroines and heroes, the dogs with jobs, without whom this book would not have been possible.

Lastly, a special thanks to Nellie, the best and most loyal friend a little girl could ever have.